Free-Form Embroidery
with Judith Baker Montano

transforming traditional stitches into fiber art

C&T PUBLISHING

PUBLISHER: **Amy Marson**

CREATIVE DIRECTOR: **Gailen Runge**

ART DIRECTOR: **Kristy Zacharias**

EDITOR: **Lynn Koolish**

COVER DESIGNER: **April Mostek**

BOOK DESIGNER: **Rose Sheifer**

PRODUCTION COORDINATOR: **Jenny Davis**

PRODUCTION EDITOR: **Alice Mace Nakanishi**

WATERCOLOR ILLUSTRATIONS: **Judith Baker Montano**

NUMBERED STITCH DIAGRAMS: **Kirstie L. Pettersen and Richard Sheppard**

Flat Embroidery Photography by C&T Publishing, Inc.;
How-to Photography by Judith Baker Montano;
Finished Fiber Artwork Photography by Robert Valentine, Giclee Print Net, Inc.,
unless otherwise noted

Published by C&T Publishing, Inc., P.O. Box 1456, Lafayette, CA 94549

Library of Congress Cataloging-in-Publication Data

Montano, Judith Baker.

Free-form embroidery with Judith Baker Montano : transforming traditional stitches into fiber art / Judith Baker Montano.

pages cm

ISBN 978-1-60705-572-3 (soft cover)

1. Embroidery. I. Title.

TT770.M635 2012

746.44--dc23

2012004062

Printed in China

10 9 8 7 6 5 4 3 2 1

Dedication

Dedicated to Paloma Boucher Montano

My little dove Paloma

Sweet baby love Paloma

Fly free and high

Throughout the sky

My little dove Paloma

Acknowledgments

Thank you to my beloved husband, Ernest Shealy, and my family, who make all the hours in the studio worthwhile. They are my beloved band of troubadours who make the journey easier.

Thank you to my editor, Lynn Koolish, and designer, Rose Sheifer, for your friendship and creative input. Along with the C&T team, you were a joy to work with.

Thank you to my wonderful friends and mentors:
Jan Beaney, Valerie Bothel, Jack Brockette, Kaffe Fassett,
Mary Fisher, Kathleen Glynn, Joan Hanley, Kathy Koch,
Dulany Lingo, Jean Littlejohn, Brandon Mabley, Penny Morgan,
Di Pettigrew, Robin Richards, Ann Riseborough, Alys Romer,
Justin Schultze, Ricky Tims, and Faye Walker.

CONTENTS

Introduction 6

Supplies and Tools 8

Threads • Ribbons • Yarns •
Fabrics • Hoops, Frames, Clamps,
and Stands • Tools • Needles •
Metric Conversions • Crochet
Hooks and Knitting Needles

Techniques 18

Choosing Background Fabrics •
Presenting Finished Pieces

Stitch Guide 23

1. Arrowhead Stitch   24

2. Arrowhead Stitch: Stacked   24

3. Backstitch: Star   25

4. Backstitch: Threaded   25

5. Braid Stitch   26

6. Bullion Stitch   26

7. Buttonhole Stitch   28

8. Buttonhole Stitch: Circle   28

9. Buttonhole Stitch: Knotted   29

10. Buttonhole Stitch:
Triangles, Half-Circles   29

11. Chain Stitch and
Chain Stitch Zigzag   30

12. Chain Stitch: Crochet   31

13. Chain Stitch: Open   31

14. Chain Stitch: Twisted   32

15. Colonial Knot   32

16. Coral Stitch   33

17. Couching Stitch   33

18. Cretan Stitch   34

19. Double Knot Stitch   35

20. Eyelet Stitch   36

21. Featherstitch:
Single / Double / Triple   36

22. Featherstitch: Leaf   37

23. Fern Leaf Stitch   38

24. Fishbone Stitch   39

25. Flat Stitch   39

26. Fly Stitch   40

27. Fly Stitch: Leaf   40

28. Fly Stitch: Seedpod   40

29. French Knot   40

30. French Knot: Couched   41

31. Head of the Bull Stitch   42

32. Herringbone Stitch   43

33. Judith's Knotted Flower
Stitch   43

34. Lazy Daisy Stitch   44

35. Leaf Ribbon Stitch   44

36. Long and Short Stitch   45

37. Loop Stitch   46

38. Maidenhair Stitch   46

39. Montano Knot   47

40. Needle Weaving Bar Stitch   47

41. Net Stitch   48

42. Overcast Stitch   49

43. Pistil Stitch   49

44. Plume Stitch   50

45. Raised Straight Stitch   50

46. Ribbon Split Stitch   51

47. Romanian Couching   52

48. Running Stitch   52

49. Satin Stitch   53

50. Scroll Stitch   54

51. Seed Stitch   54

52. Snail Trail Stitch   55

53. Spider Web Backstitch   55

54. Split Stitch   56

55. Stem Stitch   57

56. Straight Stitch   57

57. String of Pearls Stitch   58

Twisted Chain Stitch:
see 14. Chain Stitch: Twisted

58. Van Dyke Stitch   59

59. Wheat Ear Stitch and
Wheat Ear Stitch: Detached   60

60. Whipstitch: Thread and
Ribbon   61

Combining Stitches........62

ART SUPPLIES   63

TREES   64

Tree Trunks   64
Twisted Yarns and Ribbons • Silk Ribbon Stem Stitch Trunks
and Branches • Embroidered Tree Trunks and Branches •
Burned-Edge Tree Trunks • Embellished Twisted Tree

Tree Types   67
Aspen • Birch • Cypress • Evergreen / Douglas Fir •
Gum Tree / Eucalyptus • Juniper • Maple • Oak • Palm • Willow

Tree Shapes   76
Umbrella • Upright Oval • Vase • Round • Horizontal Oval •
Broad Triangle • Mound • Narrow Triangle • Narrow Upright •
Weeping • Palm • Columnar

SHRUBS   79
Prostrate • Low Spreading • Rounded Spreading • Open Spreading •
Globular • Columnar • Weeping • Pyramidal

VINES   82
Morning Glory • Ivy • Virginia Creeper • Climbing Rose •
Wisteria • Creeping Fig

GRASSES AND WEEDS   85
Blue Grama • Giant Sacaton • Indian Grass • Seagrass •
Little Bluestem • Desert Grass • Dandelion • Thistle • Tumbleweed

UNDERWATER SHAPES AND CORALS   89
Kelp • Sea Fans • Staghorn Coral • Algae • Brain Coral •
Button Coral • Anemones • Jellyfish • Starfish

BOTANICAL FLOWER SHAPES   94
Cruciform • Star • Saucer • Cup • Bell • Tubular • Funnel •
Salver • Trumpet • Rosette • Pom-Pom • Pitcher • Slipper

Think Like a Painter.......98

Light • Horizon Placement • Background • Midground •
Foreground • V and S Lines • Hints on Water •
Creating Underwater Projects • Felting

Laguna Pueblo.................114

Source Guide....................124

About the Author...........127

INTRODUCTION

Embroidery, like painting and music, is an art form steeped in traditional rules and techniques requiring years of practice. As a dyslexic I had difficulty learning from the written word, so I used pictures and diagrams. *Coats and Clark's 100 Stitches* was my best friend. After years of practice the featherstitch became second nature to me. I could eye the width and height of most stitches and I even invented some of my own stitches.

I went on to write stitch dictionaries for needleworkers using the written word, diagrams, and photographs for each stitch. They are the books I wish I had when I was learning.

With a background in traditional fine arts, I began to mix fabrics with embroidery to create landscapes and seascapes. I soon discovered that using threads, yarns, and ribbons is no different from using paint, brushes, and paper! All the traditional rules of art still apply!

I experimented with the thickness of threads and yarns, distorting the traditional stitches to create organic shapes. At first everything took on a flat folk-art look, but after rereading my basic art books things started to improve.

Many artists—such as Picasso, who studied classical art at the School of Fine Arts in Barcelona and then broke the rules with cubism, or Billy Joel, who began with a classical piano background and went on to be one of our most popular contemporary musicians—have used their classical training to produce new and innovative material. Those lessons in using gradations, and those countless hours of musical scales, paid off. They provided a good firm base from which to expand.

It is no different with the art of embroidery. Many textile artists started out with classic training as taught by the British Royal School of Embroidery, City and Guilds, or the Embroiderers' Guild, and then went on to create new avenues that forever changed and enhanced the world of needle art.

When I look back on my journey from traditional to free-form embroidery, I realize that I have many champions and influences.

Constance Howard (1920–2000), a graduate of the Royal School of Embroidery, is remembered as one of our most endearing personalities. Constance single-handedly brought embroidery into the world of art and fashion. She started the Department of Embroidery in the Art School at Goldsmiths College in London. Her vibrant personality, wild hair colors, and contagious enthusiasm made her a beloved international teacher and mentor.

Erica Wilson, an international needlework artist, was famous for her kits and patterns. As a child I waited patiently for my mother's monthly copy of *McCall's Needlework & Crafts* magazine to search out Erica's patterns and designs. Erica was born in Scotland and graduated from the Royal School of Needlework in London. She ran a successful needlework shop in New York City for 33 years, hosted two PBS embroidery shows, and has written sixteen needlework books!

One man on my list of needlework champions is Roosevelt "Rosey" Grier, a professional football player. He loved needlepoint and macramé and designed several patterns for publication. I admired him because he was such a big man (6′5″ and 300 pounds) and I could visualize him, head down over his needlepoint, in the locker room, ignoring all the taunts of his fellow players. He wrote *Rosey Grier's Needlepoint for Men* in 1973 and was a popular contributor to the needlework magazines of the time.

Annemieke Mein of Sale, Australia, is a textile artist and hero of mine. She was born in Haarlem, the Netherlands, in 1944. She immigrated with her parents to Australia in 1951. Her love of wildlife is depicted in her wide, sweeping textiles worked in minute detail on a grand scale. Annemieke was the first textile artist to be a member of the Wildlife Art Society of Australia and the Australian Guild of Realist Artists. In 1988 she received the Order of Australia medal for services to the arts. She encouraged and inspired me to attempt some of my early landscape pieces.

Pat Langford (1927–2003) of Melbourne, Australia, was a student of Constance Howard's and a wonderful artist in her own right. We met in Australia years ago and I always thought she was the consummate artist with a needle. She used her drawings and paintings to develop her needle-art projects. Pat was able to take her work from the paper and brush to the fabric and needle with an interesting mix of both media.

Kaffe Fassett, well-known designer of knitting patterns and needlework, is a friend and hero of mine. We met years ago at the Houston Quilt Show when I followed him for an autograph! Kaffe was there for his first quilt design book, and I was there as a teacher.

Kaffe studied at the School of the Museum of Fine Arts in Boston but left to paint in London, and has lived there since 1964. In 1988 he had a one-man show at London's Victoria and Albert Museum, the first time a living textile artist was featured. Kaffe has written more than 30 books and hosted many BBC television shows.

During my early teaching days in Australia, I was introduced to the work of Jan Beaney and Jean Littlejohn. We often taught in Australia at the same time, but our paths never crossed. Thanks to my dear friend and textile artist Mary Fisher, I attended a 2009 Beaney and Littlejohn seminar, my first class ever. Jan and Jean are amazing artists, and as instructors they have a lovely way of working together. This class validated my work and gave me confidence to continue with my landscape and seascape projects. Above all, I gained two lovely new friends whom I admire and respect.

Jan Beaney is an internationally recognized designer, teacher, and author. She has been a lecturer and resident artist at the Windsor School of Textile Art in East Berkshire, England, for many years. She is an honorary member of City and Guilds, for which she has served as an instructor, verifier, and examiner of embroidery for 40 years.

Jean Littlejohn is an innovative stitcher, international teacher, and author. A former vice president of the Windsor and Maidenhead Embroiderers' Guild, she has been a lecturer and resident artist at East Berkshire College since 1977. She is an honorary member of the Embroiderers' Guild and a former joint chief examiner and verifier for City and Guilds.

Jan and Jean were named Textile Teachers of the Year 2007 at the Knitting and Stitching Show in Great Britain. Together they create amazing books and DVDs through their publishing company, Double Trouble.

The aforementioned names are the key people who have influenced and inspired me on my journey with embroidery.

There are so many other wonderful contemporary textile artists to acknowledge and not enough room on this page. Such people as Pat Langford, Barbara Lee Smith, Cindy Hickock, Carol Shinn, Sherrill Kahn, Sandra Meech, Gwen Hadley, Richard Box, Verina Warren, and Wendy Lees deserve mention. Please refer to the Source Guide (page 124) for their books and websites.

It is fascinating to observe the development of free-form embroidery and textile arts, all because of Constance Howard's amazing journey. Her students have become innovative teachers and textile artists in their own right. They have traveled to and settled down in various parts of the world, producing more students who continue the journey.

So here I am, self-taught but greatly inspired by these amazing artists, all walking our individual paths but using embroidery as an art medium. This book is a stitch dictionary of free-form stitches along with watercolor illustrations from my journals for inspiration. I hope it will help you develop your own style and art form.

SUPPLIES AND TOOLS

Every good needleworker needs supplies and materials to produce her
or his artwork. Purchase the best materials you can afford—you are
worth it and working with quality materials will be a pleasure.

Threads

Many, many types of threads can be used for free-form embroidery. The weight and thickness of a thread is very important, as you will be "painting" with it. Make sure you have a selection that ranges from very fine to heavy, full threads.

Stranded cotton   This is commonly a six-stranded thread, loosely twisted and easily separated, and it comes in a skein. Use a single thread for fine work or all six strands for heavy texture. This is a versatile thread used in most types of embroidery. Brands include DMC, Anchor, Madeira, Caron, and Treenway Silks.

Stranded floss or stranded threads   Besides cotton, stranded threads come in a variety of other materials such as metallic, linen, silk, or rayon and can be four to fourteen strands. The threads can have a shiny or matte finish. Brands include Stef Francis, Color Streams, Madeira, Caron, Edmart, and Treenway Silks.

Pearl cotton   This is a tightly twisted cotton thread with a slight sheen or matte finish. It comes in solids and variegates. It is sold in sizes 3, 5, 8, 12, and 16, with 3 being the heaviest and 16 the finest. Brands include Valdani, DMC, and Anchor.

Matte or soft embroidery cotton   Also known as *coton á broder*, this five-ply twisted thread is soft and has a matte finish. It is wonderful to use for canvas and heavy fabrics. I use Anchor Soft Embroidery.

Buttonhole twist   A lustrous three-stranded silk thread on a very tight twist, this thread is traditionally used for hand-worked buttonholes. It is wonderful for traditional and free-form embroidery stitches. Brands include Treenway Silks and YLI.

Metallic threads   These threads come in a variety of weights and textures. Used in goldwork embroidery, they are very versatile for free-form embroidery. Brands include Sulky, Kreinik, Superior Threads, and YLI.

Flat threads   These threads lie flat and cannot be separated. Ribbon floss is an example of a flat thread. Options include Kreinik metallic ribbons, Neon Rays, Flair, and YLI.

Chainette threads   These threads look like a long line of crochet loops. They can be made thinner by pulling on one end. Brands include GoldRush by Rainbow Gallery and Stef Francis.

Ribbons

 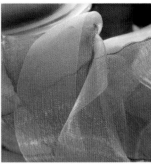

Ribbons are divided into woven and nonwoven categories. Woven ribbons are usually narrow bands of cloth with a finished edge. Nonwoven ribbons are usually made from plastic, glued and bonded, such as florist ribbons. Woven ribbons are preferable for fiber artists, as the ribbons are flexible and pliant. Free-form embroiderers use them for embroidery and surface design.

Silk   Traditional silk ribbon is woven and comes in various widths: 2mm, 4mm, 7mm, and 13mm. It is used in silk ribbon embroidery and surface techniques. Brands include Treenway Silks, YLI, Color Streams, and Spiral Dyes.

Silk bias   This is a fine silk weight that usually has a raw edge. It is best used for surface work such as weaving and couching. I use Hanah Silk.

Acetate   This is a stiff ribbon usually used in gift wrapping and the floral industry. Some of the lighter weights can be burned on the edges for an interesting texture.

Chiffon, organdy, and organza   These are better known as sheers and come in a wide variety of widths and colors. I use Mokuba ribbons.

Grosgrain   Grosgrain ribbons are usually heavier, with raised vertical ridges. Most are cotton or rayon.

Jacquard   This is a woven ribbon with shiny and matte finishes forming the design. Look on the back for a looser weave in the opposite color combination.

Moiré   Like the fabric, this is a watermarked ribbon with a satin finish.

Satin   This ribbon with a soft, smooth sheen can be double sided or single sided.

Velvet   This ribbon can be silk or polyester, with a deep pile that forms a soft velour appearance.

Wired   The French are famous for their wired ombré ribbon. It comes in a variety of widths and is used for surface work. The wire edges hold the shapes in place.

Yarns

Yarns come in many weights and are divided into worsteds and woolens. Worsted yarns are tightly twisted and use long fibers, giving a smooth finish. Woolen yarns are made of shorter fibers—the twist is looser, making them softer and bulkier.

A standard yarn weight system set by the Craft Yarn Council makes it possible for people from around the world to understand the thickness or thinness of a yarn because the system is based on numbers. It uses a scale from 1 to 6, with 1 being the finest yarn (also known as super fine) and 6 being the thickest (also known as super bulky).

Crewel yarn   This yarn comes in one or two plies. It is a fine yarn used for crewel and canvas work. Brands include Appleton and Bella Lusso Wool.

Persian yarn   This is composed of three plies of loosely twisted yarn, with one ply similar to crewel yarn in thickness and weight. Brands include Paragon and Paternayan.

Tapestry yarn or wool   This tightly twisted four-ply yarn is the most popular for crewel embroidery. Options include Elsa Williams four-ply tapestry yarn and Anchor Tapisserie.

Knitting yarns   This is a general category for many types and weights of yarn. Synthetics, silks, rayons, bamboo, and ribbons can be used for textile art. Visit weaving and knitting shops for a varied selection.

Fabrics

There are so many fabrics to choose from in textile arts, and sometimes it can be confusing. Here is a comprehensive list that will get you started. Always decide before you begin whether the project will require washing or dry cleaning.

Barkcloth   This is a cloth made from the bark of trees. The bark is beaten into a paper-thin fiber and then dyed. Mulberry bark is a popular fiber used in textile arts.

Batiste   A medium-weight plain-weave fabric, usually made of cotton or cotton blends, batiste is used in heirloom embroidery and fine needlework.

Boiled wool   This is a felted knitted wool that is flexible and warm. It can be made by washing 100% wool jersey

in hot water and drying in a hot dryer. There will be about 50% shrinkage.

Broadcloth A tightly woven plain-weave fabric, with a slight ridge effect in one direction, broadcloth is usually made from cotton or cotton/polyester blends.

Calico A tightly woven cotton fabric with an allover print, usually a small floral pattern on a contrasting background color.

Canvas This woven cotton, linen, or synthetic fabric is made with a basic plain weave in heavy- and firm-weight yarns. It is also referred to as duck.

Challis A lightweight, soft plain-weave fabric with a slightly brushed surface, the fabric is often printed, usually in a floral pattern. It is generally made of cotton, wool, or rayon.

Cheesecloth This is a lightweight, sheer, loosely woven cotton fabric with a very soft texture. It may be natural colored, bleached, or dyed. It is used for canning and jam making.

Chiffon A plain-woven lightweight, extremely sheer, airy, and soft silk, rayon, or synthetic fabric, containing highly twisted filament yarns.

Chintz A glazed plain-weave cotton fabric, chintz is often printed with brightly colored flowers or stripes. Its name comes from the Hindu word meaning "spotted." Unglazed chintz is called cretonne.

Corduroy A cotton fabric with rows of ridges, or wales, parallel to the selvage. The ridges are built so that lines can be seen when the pile is cut. Corduroy is classified by the number of wales, or cords, to the inch.

Crepe This is a lightweight fabric of silk, rayon, cotton, wool, man-made, or blended fibers, characterized by a crinkled surface.

Damask A glossy jacquard fabric (see Jacquard, at right), usually made from linen, cotton, rayon, silk, or blends. The patterns are flat and reversible. It is often used for napkins and tablecloths.

Drill A heavy, strong, durable twilled fabric of cotton or synthetic fibers, similar to denim.

Duchess satin One of the heaviest and richest-looking satins. It is usually made of silk and is also known as *peau de soie.*

Duck A tightly woven, heavy plain-weave bottom-weight fabric with a hard, durable finish, duck is usually made of cotton.

Dupioni The silk for dupioni comes from fiber formed by two silkworms spinning their cocoons together in an interlocking manner (or from single cocoons that are spun side by side and interlocked). The yarn is uneven, irregular, and larger than regular filaments. It is used to make shantung and dupioni.

Eyelet This fabric contains patterned cut-outs, around which stitching or embroidery is applied in order to prevent the fabric from unraveling.

Faille A glossy, soft, finely ribbed silklike woven fabric made from cotton, silk, or synthetics.

Felt This is a nonwoven fabric made from wool, hair, fur, or synthetic fibers. The fibers are locked together in a process using heat, water, and pressure to form a compact material.

Flannel A medium-weight plain-weave or twilled fabric usually made from cotton, cotton blends, or wool. Flannel has a very soft hand; it is brushed on both sides to create a soft, fuzzy surface.

Gabardine A tightly woven, twilled, worsted fabric with a slight diagonal line on the right side. Gabardine is made of wool, polyester, cotton, rayon, and various blends.

Gauze This is a thin, sheer plain-weave fabric made from cotton, wool, silk, rayon, or synthetic fibers. Gauze is used for curtains, apparel, trimmings, and surgical dressings.

Habutai A soft, lightweight silk dress fabric originally woven in the gum on hand looms in Japan.

Jacquard A woven fabric with a shiny or matte finish forming the woven design. Brocade and damask are types of jacquard woven fabrics.

Mousseline This is the name for a wide category of fabrics that are fairly sheer and lightweight and made in a variety of fibers. Mousseline has a crisp hand and is often used today for a fabric resembling *peau de soie* (see Duchess satin, at left).

Noil A silk fabric that has the look of hopsack but is much softer. Silk noil, sometimes called raw silk, has a nubby feel and a low sheen.

Organdy A stiffened, sheer, lightweight plain-weave fabric, organdy has a medium to high yarn count.

Organza A crisp, sheer, lightweight plain-weave fabric, with a medium to high yarn count, made of silk, rayon, nylon, or polyester. It is used primarily in evening and wedding apparel.

Satin This is a fabric with a basic weave, characterized by long floats of yarn on the face of the fabric, creating a smooth and shiny surface. Examples of satin weave fabrics include slipper satin, crêpe-back satin, faille satin, bridal satin, moleskin, and antique satin.

Tulle Tulle is a lightweight, extremely fine machine-made netting, usually with a hexagon-shaped mesh effect. It is used for veils and dance costumes.

Tussah This fabric is woven from silk fibers made by wild, uncultivated silkworms. Tussah is naturally tan in color, cannot be bleached, and has a rougher texture than cultivated silk.

Tweed A medium- to heavyweight woolen twill-weave fabric containing colored slubbed yarns.

Velour Velour is a medium-weight closely woven fabric with a thick pile. It resembles velvet but has a lower-cut pile.

Velvet Velvet is a type of tufted fabric in which the cut threads are very evenly distributed, with a short, dense pile, giving it a distinct feel. Velvet can be made from any fiber. Variations include the following:

> *Crushed velvet* is any velvet with an irregular pattern of nap going in different directions. The pattern gives the fabric a crushed or rumpled appearance.

> *Panné* is a type of lustrous, lightweight velvet fabric in which the pile has been flattened in one direction. It has a longer or higher pile than regular velvet and is often made as a knit fabric.

Velveteen A cotton cut-pile weave fabric, velveteen is woven with two sets of filling yarns; the extra set creates the pile. It has a much lower nap than velvet (above).

Voile This is a crisp, lightweight, plain-weave cottonlike fabric, made with high-twist yarns in a high-yarn-count construction. Similar in appearance to organdy (page 11) and organza (above), it is used in heirloom embroidery.

Hoops, Frames, Clamps, and Stands

I don't usually use a hoop when working on my landscapes, seascapes, and underwater scenes because I often roll the project as I am working on it. Many needleworkers prefer using a hoop, though, so I have included the following information. As with any type of artwork, use what works for you.

Handheld Embroidery Hoops

Embroidery hoops consist of two circles of wood, metal, or plastic that fit one over the other, holding the fabric in between. The hoops come in a wide variety of sizes. The downside of using a hoop is that the hoop must be held in one hand, which restricts the speed of the embroidery. Hoops will leave marks on your embroidery and background fabric, so always remove the piece from the hoop when you are not working on it.

SCREW-TIGHTENING HOOPS

Some hoops can be tightened or loosened with a screw on the outside circle. This allows you to keep the fabric tight in the hoop, with an even tension all around. Some hoops come with a plastic lip on the inside hoop for a tighter fit. Many textile artists wrap the inside circles of wooden hoops with yarn to create soft but firm tension.

PINCH-STYLE HOOPS

This style has circular metal handles that, when squeezed, allow the inside circle to fit into the outside circle. The fabric lies on the inside circle and is then tightened when the handles are released. The tension is looser with this style of hoop and needs to be adjusted frequently.

SNAP PLASTIC FRAMES

This setup comes in rectangles or squares. Plastic tubes form the frame. The fabric lies over this frame, and the holders (larger tubes cut in half and cut to a shorter length) snap over the fabric and the tubes underneath. This is a looser hold but works well on larger projects.

Embroidery Stands

An embroidery stand is simply a hoop on a stand, allowing the embroiderer to have both hands free! It usually comes in two pieces, the hoop and the stand. The hoop fits into the stand, and the height and tilt can be adjusted for ease and comfort.

The hoop can be a circle, square, or rectangle.

The hoops and stands come in wood, plastic, and metal, with wood being the most common. Some are pinch styles, in which the ends of the project are caught between two end dowels that are tightened to hold the fabric. The other style has canvas webbing attached to the end dowels. The ends of the project are basted to these canvas strips and then rolled to tighten. Some of these have a variety of dowel lengths, and the dowels can be purchased separately.

How to Choose a Hoop or Stand

Choosing a hoop or stand is really a matter of personal preference. The small handheld hoops do not require a lot of time for preparing the fabric and are good for fast and small projects. These hoops are portable and easily set up.

Embroidery stands require more preparation time but are sturdier and allow the embroiderer to carry on with a long-term project and to have the luxury of using both hands and being able to tilt the project to the back when needed.

Tools

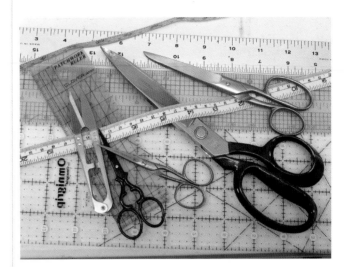

Scissors   Always keep a variety of sharpened scissors at hand, from small pointed embroidery scissors to 12″ fabric cutters and dime-store paper scissors. I keep two small embroidery scissors on my worktable, one with long slender blades and one with short pointed blades.

Rulers   A 6″ see-through ruler sits on my worktable for quick measurements. A variety of yardsticks and tapes are kept on a hook for larger projects. I keep a variety of rotary cutting rulers near my cutting board.

Tweezers   I keep a small pair of pointed tweezers in a dish on my worktable. This instrument is wonderful for picking out stitches and for picking off bits of thread from the surface of my work. I keep a long blunt-ended pair of tweezers on the dye table and another pair near the candles I use for burning edges of fabric.

Embellisher or felting machine Felting/embellisher machines hold a number of sharp barbed felting needles. These needles work up and down, pushing one fiber into another. An embellisher works like a sewing machine with the feed dogs down, and there is no thread!

I use a Baby Lock 7 needle embellisher as a holding and blending tool. I was introduced to this wonderful machine at a Jan Beaney and Jean Littlejohn seminar. It has saved me hours and hours of tacking and stitching materials into place for further embroidery stitches. I am still learning how to use this machine, and the possibilities are endless.

There are many types of embellishing machines, and many sewing machine companies offer a felting/embellishing attachment.

There is a wide variety of handheld embellishing needles, from the single needle to a plastic holder with five needles. I was introduced to felting needles in Australia and used them in some of my early pieces. The single needle is easy to use, but enthusiastic punching can hurt the holding hand, so be careful.

Irons I use a steam iron in my workroom, and I want it to be instantly steaming! I have gone through many irons in my career. I try to have the steam iron and ironing board close at hand. Most times I keep a small triangle-shaped Clover iron on my worktable for small pieces and detail ironing.

Needles

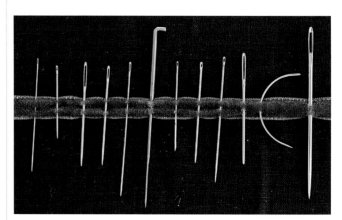

Needle varieties (*from left to right*): #10 beading, #7 between, #18 chenille, #3 crewel embroidery, #7 dollmaking, #38 felting, #5 leather (glover), #3 sharps, #3 straw (milliners), #18 tapestry, 1.5″ upholstery, #14 yarn darner

Choose your needles wisely and have a large variety to choose from. My rule is that the eye of the needle must pass through the fabric smoothly: The eye needs to be large enough to make a hole in the fabric that allows the thread to pass through smoothly without snagging or catching.

Needles are sized by numbers, and the higher the number, the finer the needle. Quality does vary and makes a difference in your work. My preferred brands are John James, Piece Makers, S. Thomas and Sons, and Mary Arden of England.

HAND-SEWING NEEDLE TYPES

NEEDLE		TYPICAL SIZES	USAGE
Beading	Very long, fine needle with a narrow eye	10–15	Narrow enough for small beads and long enough to load with many beads to be threaded at one time
Between (quilting)	A short, fine needle with a round eye	3–12	Best for quilting and other fine stitching
Bodkin	Long, thick needle with a ball-point end and a long eye	3"–6"	Can be flat or round; use for threading ribbon, elastic, or lace; good for weaving
Chenille	A thick, pointed needle with an elongated, large eye	13–28	Suitable for thick thread such as crewel yarn and six-stranded floss; ideal for ribbon and wool embroidery
Crewel embroidery	A finer needle with a large, long eye for easier threading	3–10	All-purpose needle for fine embroidery using up to six-stranded threads
Dollmaking	A long needle with a large, smooth eye and a strong shaft	3"–7"	Good for stitching through thick layers (some of my foregrounds are 4" thick when I'm done)
Felting	A 3" shaft of gauged wire with barbs and a sharp tip	36–42	Use for hand felting, embellishments, meshing, and layering
Leather (glover)	Comes in a variety of lengths, with a triangle-shaped tip; also called a wedge needle	3/0–10	Use for piercing leather, plastic, suede, Ultrasuede, and other heavy fabrics
Sharps	An all-purpose medium-length needle with a round eye	3–12	Good for appliqué, quilting, and bullion knots
Straw (milliners)	A long, fine needle with a tiny eye no wider than the shaft	1–11	Good for bullion knots and beading; originally used for hat making
Tapestry	A medium-length needle with a thick shaft, blunt tip, and long eye	13–28	Use for cross-stitch, blackwork, Hardanger, and wool and ribbon embroidery
Upholstery (curved)	A curved needle with a large eye	1½"–6"	Use for box making or sewing difficult areas; also good for heavy yarns
Yarn darner	A long, strong needle with a heavy shaft	14–18	Use for heavy yarns

Sewing Machine Needle Sizes

The European needle size is the actual size of the needle shaft in hundredths of a millimeter. The American size is just an assigned number and not the actual size.

EUROPEAN NUMBER	AMERICAN NUMBER
60	8
65	9
70	10
75	11
80	12
90	14
100	16
110	18
120	19

Metric Conversions

The old adage of measure twice and cut once is so true. Below is a ruler with both inches and centimeters and a conversion chart to help simplify the mystery of inches, millimeters, centimeters, and meters.

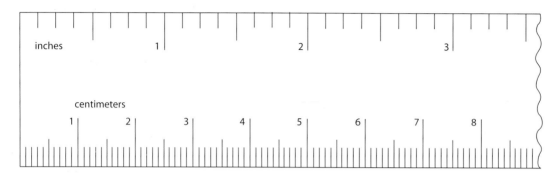

In the metric system, everything is done in multiples of 10. I have memorized this little verse for myself:

There are 10 millimeters in 1 centimeter and 100 millimeters in 10 centimeters and 100 centimeters in 1 meter. There are 10 centimeters in 3.93 inches and 1 meter equals 39.3 inches.

LENGTH CONVERSIONS

INCHES	MILLIMETERS	CENTIMETERS
¹⁄₁₆″	1.6mm	
⅛″	3mm	
¼″	6.3mm	
½″	12.7mm	
¾″	19mm	
1″	25.4mm	2.54cm
6″		15.24cm
12″		30.48cm
39.37″		100.00cm (1 meter)

FEET	YARDS	METERS
1′		0.30m
2′		0.61m
3′	1 yard	0.91m
6′	2 yards	1.83m

Crochet Hooks and Knitting Needles

I do use crochet hooks and knitting needles in my textile art. Sometimes I use a knitted shape to create texture. I use the crochet hooks to create long dimensional chain-link lines in landscape and underwater projects.

Below are the size charts, with metric (mm), old British (UK), and U.S. sizes.

CROCHET HOOK SIZES

METRIC (MM)	OLD UK SIZE	U.S. SIZE
0.60	6	14
—	5½	13
0.75	5	12
—	4½	11
1.00	4	10
—	3½	9
1.25	3	8
1.50	2½	7
1.75	2	6
—	1½	5
2.00	1	4
2.25	13	B/1
2.50	12	—
2.75	—	C/2
3.00	11	—
3.25	10	D/3
3.50	9	E/4
3.75	—	F/5
4.00	8	G/6
4.50	7	7
5.00	6	H/8
5.50	5	I/9
6.00	4	J/10

KNITTING NEEDLE SIZES

METRIC (MM)	OLD UK SIZE	U.S. SIZE
2	14	0
2.25	13	1
2.75	12	2
3	11	3
3.25	10	4
3.75	9	5
4	8	6
4.5	7	7
5	6	8
5.5	5	9
6	4	10
6.5	3	—
7	2	10½
7.5	1	—
8	0	11
9	00	13
10	000	15
12	—	17½
15	—	19

TECHNIQUES

Choosing Background Fabrics

Refer to Fabrics (pages 10–12) as needed.

I choose my background fabrics very carefully for embroidery projects. The background fabric acts as a foundation, providing texture and color to complement the chosen threads and yarns.

Over the years I have developed a color chart that helps my students in crazy quilting, embroidery, and textile arts. I break the tones of color down to five categories to make it easier to make good choices using complementary colors, mood, and extender colors. In choosing the background color for a project I use the extender colors from the Montano Color Theory chart.

I use this chart to create the mood or feel for land- and seascapes. The lighter the tone of color, the airier and sunnier the piece becomes. The dusty tones create moods from hazy to stormier land- and seascapes. Anything in shadows uses dusty tones. I use jewel tones to create the dramatic feel and mood for underwater projects.

Pastels (Light)

Pastel colors are very soft and pale. Lots of white has been added to the pure color. Red becomes pink, purple becomes lavender, yellow becomes cream, and so on. Background colors best used for a pastel palette are white and cream. Because the pastel colors have a light, soft, baby, or feminine feel, look for fabrics that have a soft sheen, a slight jacquard pattern, or a moiré watermark. Use this palette to create landscapes with a lot of light, sunshine, and air.

MONTANO COLOR THEORY

PAINT				
Light	**Light Medium**	**Medium**	**Dark Medium**	**Dark**
Add white to pure paint.	Add a little black to white paint.	Add more black to white paint to darken.	Add only black.	Create deep contrast.

FABRIC				
Pastel	**Light Dusty**	**Dusty**	**Dark Dusty**	**Jewel Tones**
Soft	Desert	Old	Rembrandt	Mardi Gras
Baby	Hazy	Worn	Antique	Fireworks
Feminine	Patina	Foggy	Victorian	Dramatic
Sweet	Tea stain	Stormy	Moody	Neon lights

EXTENDERS OR BACKGROUND				
White	Cream	Dark cream	Black	Black
Cream	Light gray	Medium gray	Dark gray	
	Taupe	Dark taupe		
		Khaki		

HIGHLIGHTS				
Silver	Silver	Silver	Silver	Silver
	Light gold	Medium gold	Old gold	Old gold
				Rust orange

Light Dusty (Light Medium)

Light dusties are pastel colors that have a bit of black added to them to create a soft grayed and muted effect. Words such as *hazy*, *muted*, *desert*, and *patina* best describe this group. The best background colors for a light dusty project are cream, light gray, and taupe. Make sure the texture of the fabric is not too rough, as it will compete with the needlework. Use this palette to create desert scenes or rainy days and hazy seascapes.

Dusty (Medium)

At this point more black is added than white to the pure colors. It creates a moodier feeling using grayed tonal shades. Words to describe this are *old*, *worn*, *foggy*, and *stormy*. Good background colors are medium gray, dark taupe, dark cream, and khaki. Look for matte finishes when choosing the fabrics. Create stormy and foggy scenes using this palette.

Dark Dusty (Dark Medium)

For these colors, the painter adds only black to the pure colors. This creates a deeply moody, Victorian feel to the project. Words that best describe this are *antique*, *Rembrandt*, *Victorian*, and *moody*. Black and darkest gray are the best background colors. Depending on the needlework subject, choose a fabric texture that will not compete. Create dark, moody landscapes with this palette.

Jewel Tones (Dark)

If the painter continues to add black, the color will become muddied and dull, but think of jungle flowers, neon lights, Mardi Gras, and fireworks! These are the jewel tone colors that create drama and excitement. The only background for jewel tone colors is black, as it will always make the colors appear more vibrant. These colors are wonderful for underwater scenes.

Presenting Finished Pieces

There are many ways to present finished textile projects. I always try to answer a few basic questions before I make this decision.

- Will this project be washable?
- How much wear and tear will this project endure?
- How will I clean this project if it gets dusty?
- How much am I willing to spend on the presentation of this project?

Wallhanging

Many textile art projects can be backed with fabric and a presentation sleeve so the finished project can hang from a rod on the wall. This is a relatively inexpensive way to present your work. Just make sure it hangs out of direct light and in a place where it won't be touched.

Stitched to Canvas

Some textile art projects can be presented on prepared oil painting canvases, or you can buy wooden stretcher bars to create your own sizes of canvas. I use a background fabric that complements the project and is easy to sew through. The fabric is then stapled to the wooden form and a hanging wire is added to the back. Make sure the finished project has been properly sized—I do this by drawing the outline of the final size of the piece on foamcore board and pulling and stretching as needed until the piece is the correct size. If it's okay to get the piece damp, I spritz it with water before sizing. Either way, pin the piece and leave it for several days.

Framed

I prefer to present my work like a textile painting and frame the finished piece in a mat and frame using museum-quality nonglare glass. I try to buy the best I can afford, as I feel the finishing and presentation of an art piece makes or breaks a project. I always choose a double mat because I can add spacers between the two mats to get the desired depth so the glass does not touch the fabrics. Sometimes the depth of a textile art piece can be as great as four inches!

Framing is the most expensive but the safest way to present your artwork. The textile project is stretched and wedged into a double mat and behind glass. It will not get dusty and it will never need cleaning.

MATS AND FRAMES IN THE STUDIO

I keep a big selection of working mats and frames in my studio. I use these in the development of my projects.

I decide on a finished size and then choose a mat with that inside measurement. The mat may be two long L shapes taped to the proper size. I then use the mat for measuring and marking the outside lines on the background fabric of my project (using a water-erasable pen). I also use the mat as a frame to block out the outside bits that distract from the project. This way I can concentrate on the project. The mat lets me know right away if the horizon placement is working. It also allows me to see if the background is setting back into the picture or if the shading is correct.

I also use a frame around the mat when tacking my project up on the corkboard. I leave it overnight so that it is the first thing I see in the morning. Any mistakes will show right away.

Matting Your Finished Projects

1. Choose the finished size. Standard sizes of the openings are 4″ × 6″, 5″ × 7″, 8″ × 10″, 9″ × 12″, 11″ × 14″, 16″ × 20″, 18″ × 24″, and up. Make sure the finished project is ½″ bigger than the opening all around so it can be glued onto the first mat.

2. Purchase the double mat and a piece of foamcore board to be cut into strips to act as spacers between the 2 mats. Cover the outside mat and put it aside to keep it clean.

3. Lay a bead of glue on the back of the inside mat along the inside edge. I use Aleen's Tacky Glue.

4. Place the finished project into the inside mat and tape along 2 sides with masking tape. Pull the remaining sides drum tight and tape as you go. Allow the glue to dry thoroughly.

5. Cut 2 pieces of a very dense fleece, such as Pellon fleece, exactly the same size as the inside opening. Cut a third piece of fleece ¼"–½" larger than the opening.

6. Place the larger fleece precisely on the back of the finished project, making sure it overlaps the opening edges of the inside mat. Place the 2 remaining pieces precisely along the opening edges. This acts as padding, and the larger overlapping one makes the edges smoother.

7. Spread glue all over the back of the inside mat, making sure it goes right up to the edge of the fleece. Place the backing (foamcore board or cardboard) onto the mat and turn it over.

8. Cover with a cloth or tea towel and stack heavy books on the inside mat. Make sure the books are right up to the edge of the inside matte. Leave for 24 hours to ensure tight padding and no slippage.

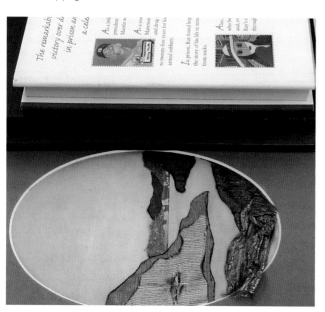

9. Place the foamcore strips in place and glue on the top mat. Make sure the depth is great enough that the glass will not touch the finished piece. You may need to add another layer of foamcore strips.

10. Take the prepared double-matted project to a framer and choose the frame and nonglare glass. The frame can be traditional, contemporary, wide, thin, wood, or metal. The choice of a frame is a very serious decision, as it can make or break the project. I always try to make the mat and the frame blend together as a unit. Try to choose the best-quality nonglare glass possible—I always use museum quality.

STITCH GUIDE

Please refer to my books *Elegant Stitches*, *Floral Stitches*, and
the *Embroidery & Crazy Quilt Stitch Tool* for left-handed
instructions for the stitches.

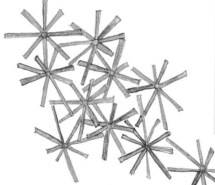

Stitches 1–5

2. Arrowhead Stitch: Stacked

From sheaths of wheat to leaf shapes, this stitch is perfect for distortion. Stack the stitches in a variety of shapes for texture.

1   Come up at A, go down at B, and then come up at C.

2   Go down at B and come up at D.

3   Continue until each arrowhead is completed, keeping the stitches evenly spaced.

Arrowhead Stitch: Leaf

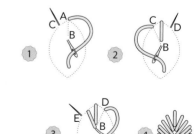

1   Mark the shape as a guide. Come up at A, go down at B, and then come up at C.

2–4   Continue working in this manner, keeping the stitches very close.

1. Arrowhead Stitch

This easy stitch can be worked in fine metallic threads for stars or sun reflections on the ocean, and in yarn for underwater anemones and seashells.

1   Come up at A, go down at B, and then come up at C.

2–3   On the return pass, work the stitches in the same way, filling in the spaces. Use this stitch on its own or stack it (at right) to make a filler stitch.

3. Backstitch: Star

With uneven straight stitches, the backstitch star can act as filler, texture, or overlay to add interest. Think stars, flowers, and underwater debris.

1   Come up at A and go down at B (point B becomes the center pivot of the stitch). Continue stitching the spokes (6 or 8), keeping them of equal length and spaced evenly.

2–3 Connect the spokes with straight stitches on the edges.

4. Backstitch: Threaded

A free-form threaded backstitch is fast and easy. Changing thread and yarn choices gives the stitches a new look. From tree branches to underwater coral, this stitch is very effective.

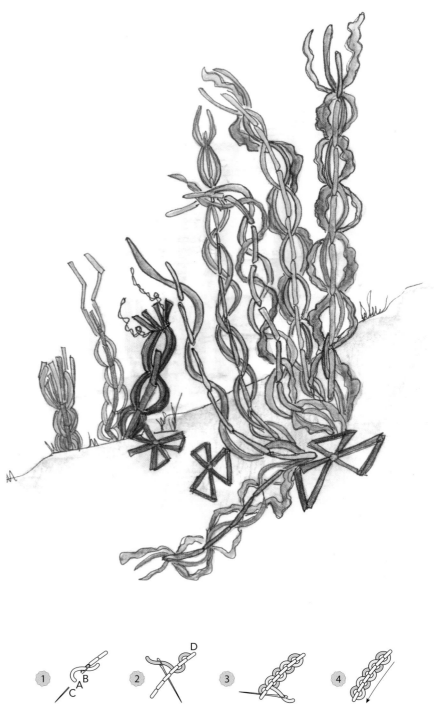

1   Come up at A, take a small backstitch to B, and then come back up at C.

2   Work the backstitches to the length desired. Come up at D with a contrasting thread. Slide the needle under the backstitches, alternating above and below the row without catching the fabric.

3–4 Interweave another contrasting thread to complete the loops.

5. Braid Stitch

This is a wonderful stitch for creating grain shapes, flowers, stems, leaves, and texture. It can be stitched side by side to create bark texture for tree trunks.

1   Come up at A, go down at B, and then come up at C. Slide the needle under the straight stitch between A and B, go down again at D (as close to C as possible, but not into it), and come back up at E.

2–3   Slide the needle under the straight stitch again, go down at F, and come up at G.

4–5   Slide the needle under the chain stitches and continue with the next stitch.

6. Bullion Stitch

This traditional stitch can be pushed into various shapes to make cactus, seaweed, tree branches, and ferns. Heavier yarns and threads create wonderful foreground shapes.

1   Decide the width of the stitch and then come up at A. Pull the thread through. Go down at B. Come up again at A.

2   Raise the tip of the needle by holding it in your left hand and putting pressure on top of the needle eye. Wrap the needle clockwise with the thread; pull the wrap firmly down toward the fabric.

3 Work the desired number of wraps until the wraps are the same width as the space from A to B. Pull the wraps firmly into place.

4 Hold the wraps and pull the needle through the wraps. Pull the thread through, holding firmly, and pull away from yourself in order to tighten the knot. Go back into B to put the bullion into place.

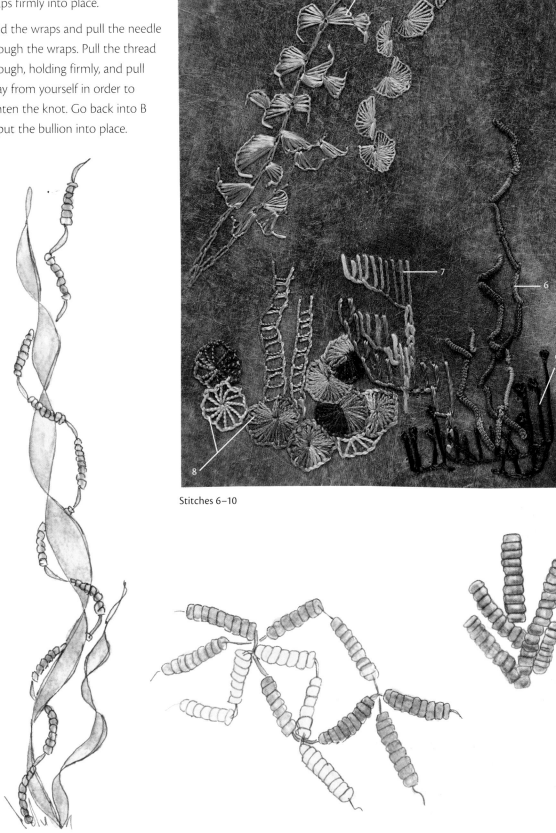

Stitches 6–10

7. Buttonhole Stitch

Work buttonhole stitches in overlapping rows for grass fields. Stack them for texture on the sides of buildings. Elongate the stitches to make sea corals.

8. Buttonhole Stitch: Circle

Work in circles for floral shapes or in uneven shapes to create seashells and anemones. Add texture and detail by changing the thread weights.

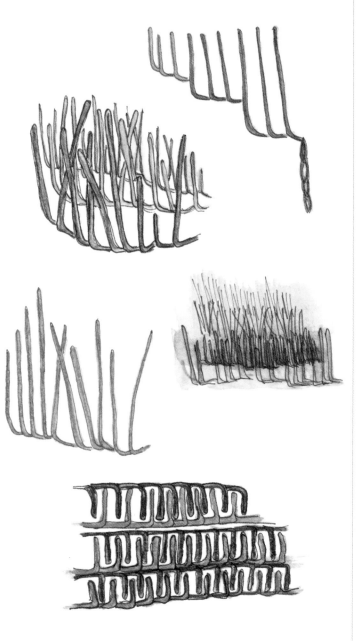

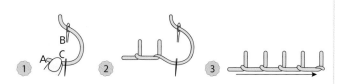

1   Come up at A, hold the thread down with your thumb, go down at B, and then come up at C.

2–3 Bring the needle tip over the thread and pull into place. Repeat.

1   Draw a circle the desired size of the flower. Bring the needle up at A (the outside of the circle). Go down at center B and come up at C, to the right of A. Make sure the needle is over the thread; pull firmly.

2–4 Continue around the circle until it is filled.

9. Buttonhole Stitch: Knotted

By distorting the knotted buttonhole you can create plant and floral shapes. Cluster and overlap this stitch to create depth.

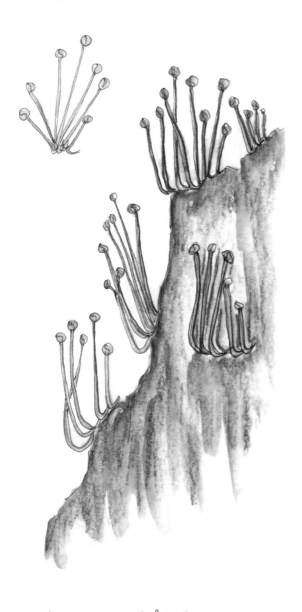

1   Come up at A and form a loop, wrapping the thread around your thumb. Slip the needle under the front of the loop.

2–3   Work the loop onto the needle. Insert the needle at B and come up at C; form a neat knot by gently tightening the loop before pulling the needle through the fabric.

10. Buttonhole Stitch: Triangles, Half-Circles

Work with variegated threads and yarns to create textural floral shapes. Place them on a straight line or let them fly free.

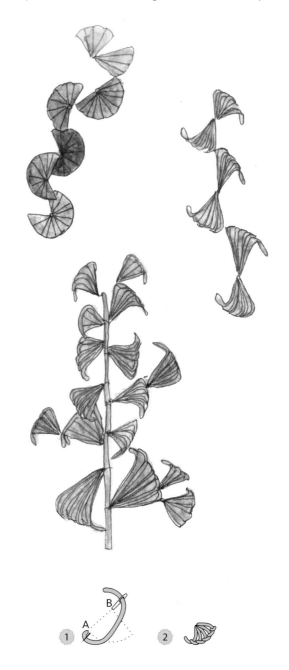

1   Draw a quarter-circle shape. Come up at A (at the outer left corner). Go down at B and bring the needle back up close to A. Loop the thread under the needle; pull through.

2   Continue making stitches to fill the area. End with a catch stitch.

Variation

Chain Stitch Zigzag

1–3 Repeat Steps 1 and 2 of Chain Stitch, but make each subsequent stitch at a 90° angle from the previous stitch.

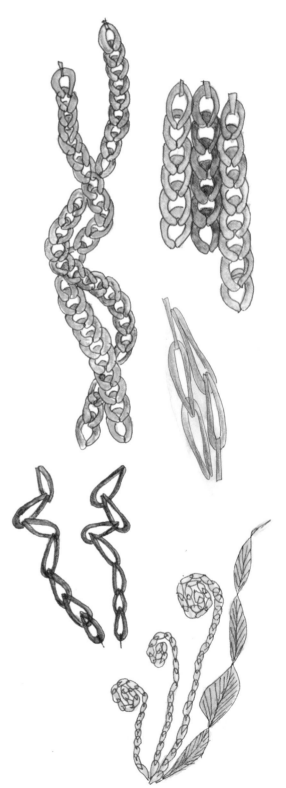

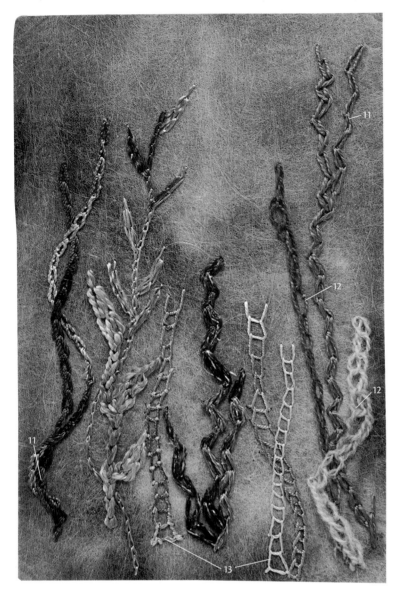

Stitches 11–13

11. Chain Stitch and Chain Stitch Zigzag

This is a great stitch for lines and texture. Stack these stitches side by side to create tree bark or work in spirals to create ferns. Play with long and short stitches in one line for a more organic look.

1–2 Come up at A and form a loop. Go down at B (as close to A as possible, but not into it) and come back up at C, bringing the needle tip over the thread. Repeat this stitch to make a chain.

12. Chain Stitch: Crochet

The crochet stitch sits on the surface to create texture and depth. Cluster rows or loop them to create organic shapes. Twine fine and thick threads for more depth.

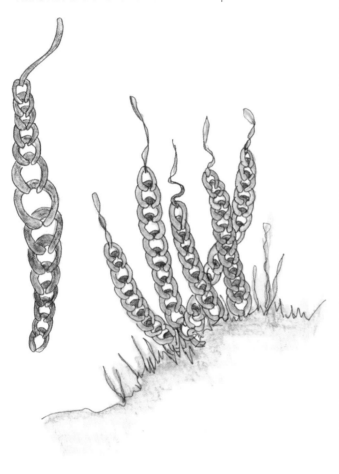

1 Come up at A, go down at B, and then come up at A again.

2–3 Remove the needle from the thread. With a crochet hook, reach under the straight stitch and work up a series of chain stitches. Work each to the desired length. Rethread the needle and anchor to the back. The chain stitch can be tacked down with another thread.

Variation

13. Chain Stitch: Open

A contemporary look is achieved with side-by-side open chain stitches. Change the color and size of thread for more interest. Think spider webs and texture on flat surfaces.

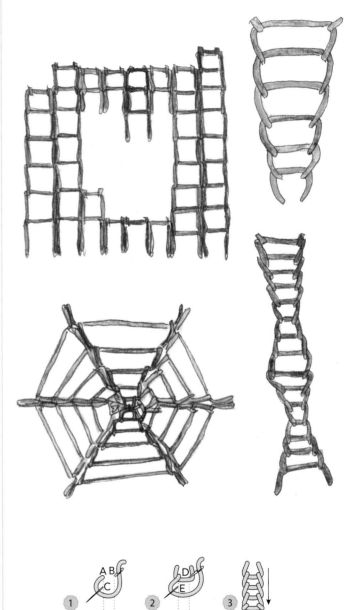

1 Work this stitch along 2 parallel lines. Come up at A and form a loop. Go down at B, even with and to the right of A, and then come up at C, bringing the needle tip over the thread. Leave the loop loose.

2–3 Go down at D, cross over the loop, and come up at E for the next stitch. Anchor the stitch end with 2 catch stitches.

14. Chain Stitch: Twisted

Also called Twisted Chain Stitch.* This stitch is similar to the snail trail stitch (page 55), but the top of the stitch is worked closer together. Use this stitch for seaweed, shrubs, and texture.

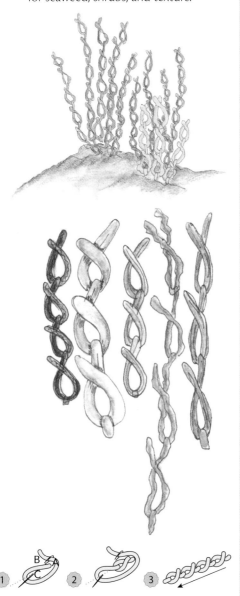

1 Work this stitch along a line. Come up at A along the designated line and form a loop. Go down at B, slightly to the left of A, and take a small, slanting stitch to C, bringing the needle tip over the thread.

2–3 Repeat this stitch for a continuous row.

* For a photo of Stitch 14, see page 58.

15. Colonial Knot

Cluster colonial knots in variegated threads and yarns to create flower heads, anemones, and rocky texture. Use fine threads for detail and heavy yarns for texture.

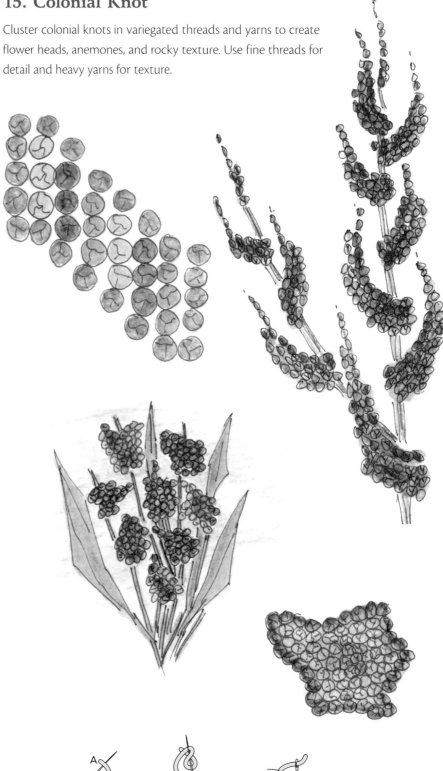

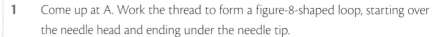

1 Come up at A. Work the thread to form a figure-8-shaped loop, starting over the needle head and ending under the needle tip.

2–4 Hold the needle upright and pull the thread firmly around the needle. Insert the needle at B (as close to A as possible, but not into it). Hold the knot in place until the needle is pulled completely through the fabric.

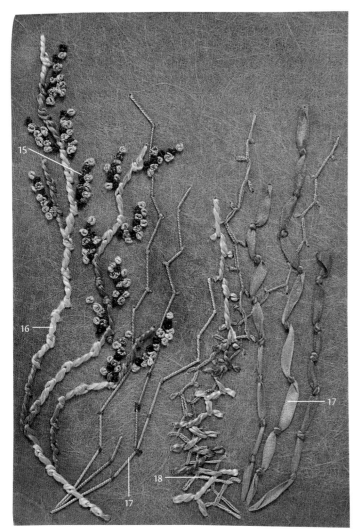

Stitches 15–18

17. Couching Stitch

This is a wonderful stitch for creating lines and texture. Use with fine threads or up to 4mm silk ribbon. Make interesting seaweed and kelp with ribbon and couched yarn.

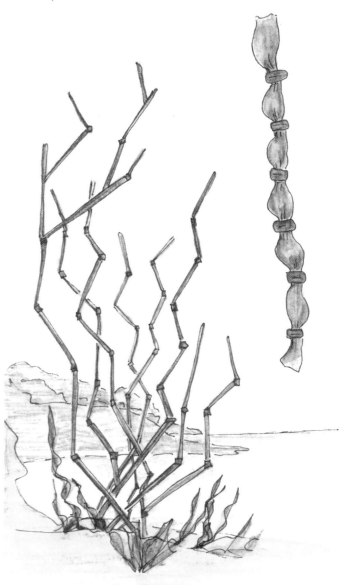

16. Coral Stitch

This is a great stitch for creating shapes such as branches, corals, twigs, shrubs, and grasses. Overlay the stitches for more depth.

1–3 Work the stitch along a designated line. Come up at A and lay the thread along the designated line. Bring the needle down at a right angle to the thread at B and come up at C, bringing the needle tip over the thread.

1–2 Couching is a decorative way to hold long (placed) threads in position. Mark a line the designated length of the couching stitch. Position the thread along the designated line. With either matching or contrasting thread or ribbon, come up at A and go down at B, wrapping a small, tight stitch over the placed thread at regular intervals.

18. Cretan Stitch

Work this stitch loosely for fence lines and seaweed or scrunch it up for fish shapes. The cretan is a very versatile stitch. Overlap the stitches for more texture.

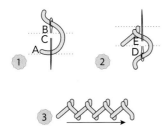

1   Work this stitch along 2 parallel lines. Come up at A, go down at B, and then come up at C, taking a downward vertical stitch and bringing the needle tip over the thread.

2–3   Go down at D and then come up at E.

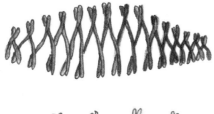

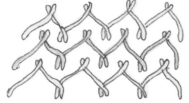

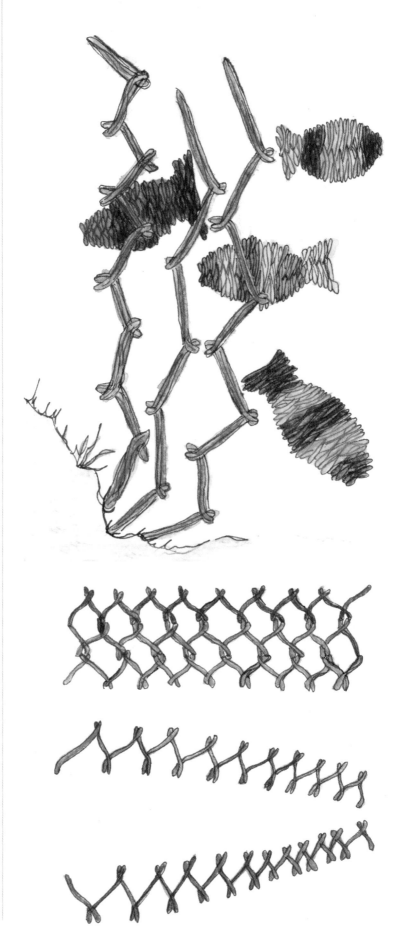

Stitches 19–23

19. Double Knot Stitch

Work the double knots close together for texture and farther apart to create branches, stems, and sea algae.

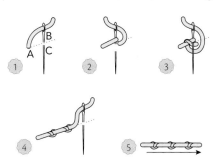

1 Work this stitch along a designated line. Come up at A, go down at B, and then come up at C.

2–3 Slide the needle under the stitch and loop the thread around the stitch, bringing the needle tip over the threads.

4–5 Pull the thread to form the knot and continue with the next stitch.

20. Eyelet Stitch

Create eyelet sea anemones, starfish, and seashells. Work the stitches into floral shapes or overlap them to create depth.

1. Gently pierce a hole in the fabric with an awl. Come up at A and then go down into the center hole.

2. Come up again and work straight stitches around the center hole. Pull firmly to keep the hole open.

21. Featherstitch: Single / Double / Triple

This is my favorite stitch because it can be stacked, overlapped, and worked in singles, doubles, and triples. It is wonderful for trees, shrubs, grasses, seaweed, and texture.

Featherstitch: Single

1. Come up at A, go down at B—even with and to the left of A—and then come up at C. The needle always lies over the thread.

2–3. Alternate the stitches back and forth, working them downward in a vertical column.

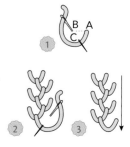

Featherstitch: Double

Work the double featherstitch in the same manner, but complete 2 stitches before alternating the direction. Stitches 1 and 3 are on the line; stitches 2 and 4 swing out.

Featherstitch: Triple

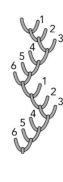

Work the triple featherstitch in the same manner, but complete 3 stitches before alternating the direction. Stitches 1 and 4 are on the line; stitches 2, 3, 5 and 6 swing out.

22. Featherstitch: Leaf

Create a large variety of leaves by distorting the stitch lengths and widths. Make the stitches textural by using yarns and silk ribbons.

1 Draw a leaf outline on the fabric. Start at the top of the leaf with the first featherstitch (previous page). Alternate the stitches left and right, working them downward in a vertical column.

2 Work out to the outside lines. These stitches are uneven and meant to be free-form. This stitch can also be worked in multiple layers of color.

Variation

23. Fern Leaf Stitch

This stitch is similar to the featherstitch but more angular. It is good for overlapping to create depth and texture in grasses and shrubs.

1 Mark a line the designated length of the fern leaf. Come up at A, go down at B (making a straight stitch), and then come up again at A.

2 Go down at C and then come up again at A.

3–4 Go down at D, keeping the length of the straight stitches consistent with the first set. Come up at E and continue with the next stitch, forming the stitch along the designated line.

Stitches 24–30

24. Fishbone Stitch

This stitch can be worked very tightly for a raised effect or very loosely to create organic shapes.

1   Draw a leaf outline on the fabric. Come up at A on the centerline. Go down at B and then come back up at C, keeping the thread on the right side of the needle.

2   Pull the thread through. With the thread on the left, go down at D and then come up at E.

3–4   Continue stitching to form the leaf.

25. Flat Stitch

I use this stitch to create little seashells, sea debris, floral shapes, and even fruit!

1. Mark 2 lines down the center of the shape as a guide for the stitches. Come up at A, go down at B, slip the needle tip under the fabric, and then come up at C.

2–3. Continue working, keeping the stitches close together and alternating from side to side. Each new stitch will overlap the base of the previous stitch.

26. Fly Stitch

The fly stitch is wonderful for landscape shapes such as grasses, shrubs, and trees. Elongate the stitches to create texture.

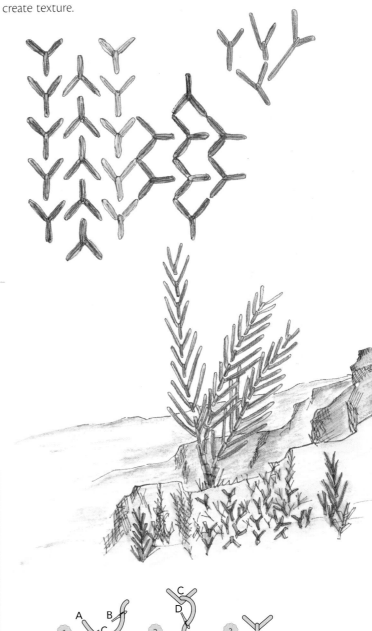

1. Come up at A, go down at B—even with and to the right of A—and then come up at C, bringing the needle tip over the thread.

2–3. Draw the thread gently through the fabric. Go down at D, forming a catch stitch.

This stitch may be worked singly or in rows.

Variation

27. Fly Stitch: Leaf

Use this stitch to create leaves, grain heads, and flowers. The result depends on the chosen weight and color of the threads.

1. Draw a leaf outline on the fabric. Make a fly stitch: Come up at A, go down at B, come up at C, and go down at D.

2. Work a series of free-form fly stitches, going to the outside edges of the leaf. The center, or spine, of the leaf will be where the catch stitch (D) of the fly stitch is placed.

28. Fly Stitch: Seedpod

I love to make seedpods from single fly stitches. Depending on the color of threads it can be dandelions, verbena florets, or any type of pod.

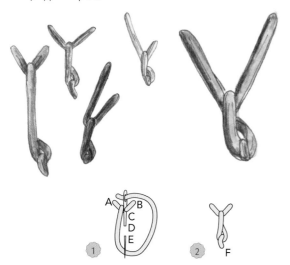

1. Work up a fly stitch (Step 1, page 39) from points A to C.

2. Hold the thread to the left. Make a small lazy daisy stitch (page 44). Go down at D and then come up at E. Pull the stitch into place, making sure the needle lies over the thread. Anchor with a catch stitch at F.

29. French Knot

I use French knots to create fine texture in underwater projects. Use them in lines or cluster them together for floral shapes.

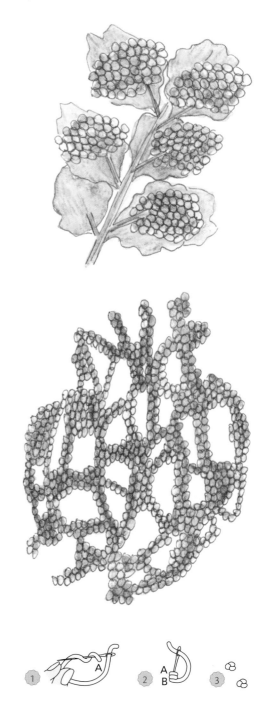

1. Come up at A and wrap the thread twice around the needle.

2–3. Holding the thread taut, go down at B (as close to A as possible, but not into it). Hold the knot in place until the needle is completely through the fabric.

30. French Knot: Couched

This is a favorite of mine for underwater projects. The knots can be barnacles or clustered on long straight stitches for seaweed. They can also provide texture on a tree trunk.

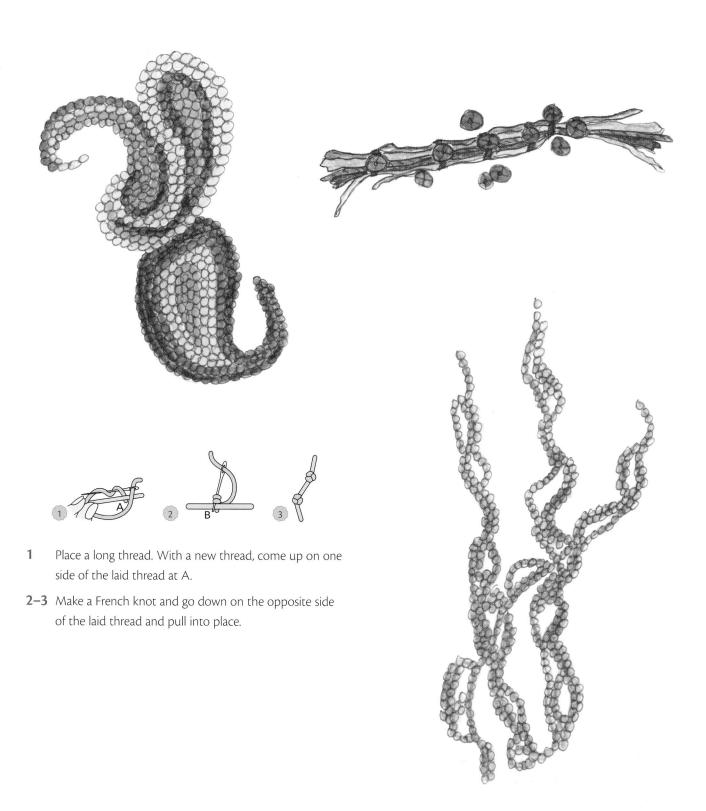

1   Place a long thread. With a new thread, come up on one side of the laid thread at A.

2–3 Make a French knot and go down on the opposite side of the laid thread and pull into place.

Stitches 31–35

31. Head of the Bull Stitch

Cluster this stitch for texture or elongate the stitch lengths for grass, seaweed, and flowers. Once again, variegates and different thread weights work wonders!

1   Come up at A, go down at B, and then come up at C, bringing the needle tip over the thread.

2   Go down at D to the right of the working thread and then come up at E, bringing the needle tip over the thread.

3–4 Take a small stitch at F to anchor the loop.

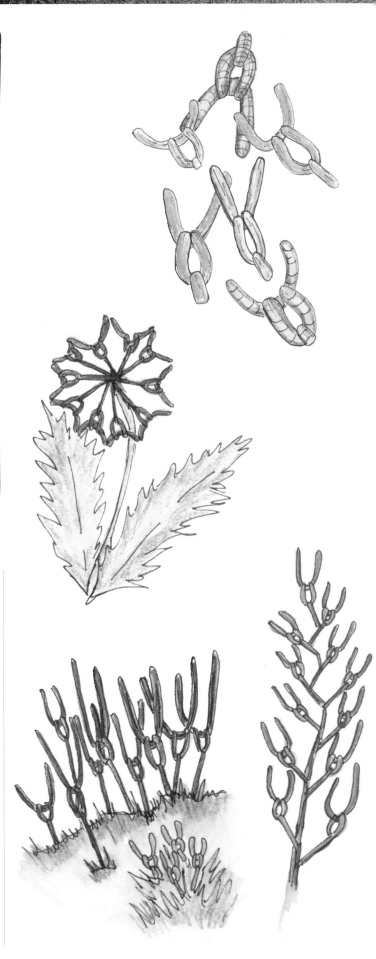

32. Herringbone Stitch

Think of crosshatching lines when using the herringbone stitch. Work this stitch in layers to create shadows and depth.

1   Come up at A, go down at B, and then come up at C.

2–3   Go down at D and then come up at E. Continue working, alternating from top to bottom.

33. Judith's Knotted Flower Stitch

I use this versatile little stitch to create lichen, anemones, moss, and texture. Cluster the stitches together for organic shapes; vary the lengths for more interest.

1   Draw a flower outline on the fabric. Use about 12″ of 4mm silk ribbon and a chenille needle. Come up at A.

2   Make a knot at the desired height (¼″ to ½″). With the needle tip, work the knot into place to tighten. Go down at A.

3–4   Come up again near A and use the needle as a laying tool to make sure both sides of the knot are even. Repeat the process until the area is filled.

34. Lazy Daisy Stitch

This is a simple stitch but very effective! Use long and short stitches to create grass, shrubs, and ground cover. Vary the thread and yarn weights for extra depth.

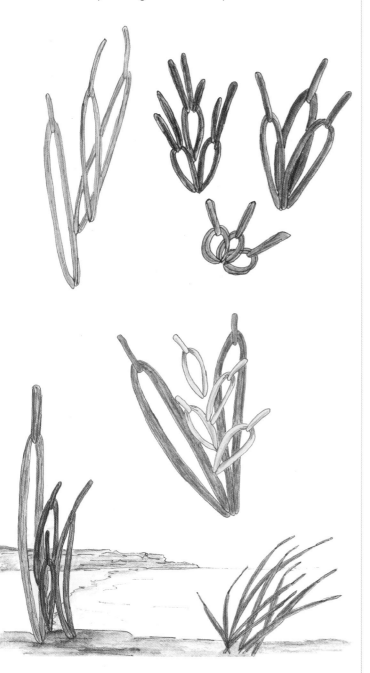

1. Come up at A and form a loop. Go down at B (as close to A as possible, but not into it) and then come up at C, bringing the needle tip over the thread.

2–3. Go down at D, making a small anchor stitch.

35. Leaf Ribbon Stitch

This is a wonderful leaf and seaweed stitch that is usually worked in silk ribbon. I like to use heavy, textural yarns and rayon threads.

1. Mark a line the desired length of the leaf. Come up at A and go down at B, forming a straight stitch, and then come up at C.

2–4. Go down at D, to the right and even with C, and come up at E, bringing the needle tip over the ribbon. Go down at F, forming a small anchor stitch. Continue with the next stitches, flaring out wider and wider to form a leaf.

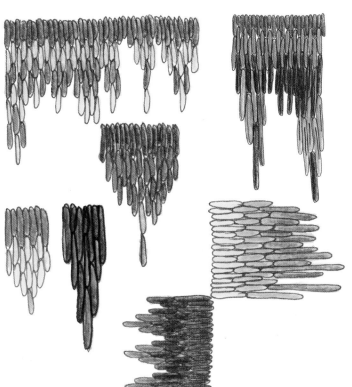

Stitches 36–39

36. Long and Short Stitch

This is best known as a Bargello stitch, but I use it for seaweed and kelp. You can form flower petals and fan corals by alternating colors and thread weights.

1   Mark the shape as a guide for the stitches. Come up at A and go down at B, making a straight stitch the desired length, and then come up at C.

2   Work the first row in alternating long and short satin stitches, keeping the outline of the shape even and defined.

3–4   Work the remaining satin stitch rows in equal lengths; vary the thread color to add shading. Use this stitch for shading or filling in large areas.

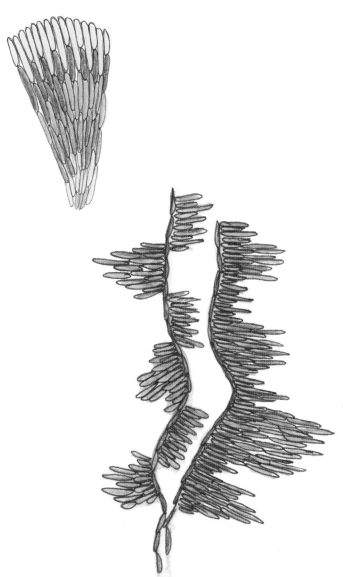

37. Loop Stitch

Use heavy yarns and silk ribbon to create this fast and easy stitch. I use it for ground cover in landscapes and for sea anemones and algae.

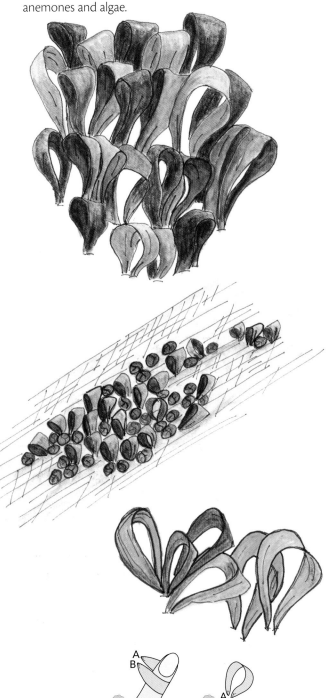

38. Maidenhair Stitch

Overlap the maidenhair stitches from very small to large to create shrubs and seaweed. Use long lengths of small, tight stitches or widen the stitch for a sweeping effect.

1–2   Using 4mm silk ribbon, come up at A and go back down at B. Use your finger or a laying tool to prevent the loop from twisting. Gently pull the loop to the desired length.

Work the loops close together. Use caution, as this stitch is easily pulled out.

1   Come up at A, go down at B, and come up at C, bringing the needle tip over the thread.

2–3   Work 3 single featherstitches (page 36) on one side, graduating the length of the stitches and aligning them vertically. Work a similar group of stitches on the opposite side.

39. Montano Knot

Work this knot in silk ribbon for floral shapes, underwater corals, and anemones.

1–2 Come up at A and loosely wrap the thread around the needle (wrap 1 to 6 times, depending on the desired size). Insert the needle back into the fabric (as close to A as possible, but not into it). Pull through, but do not hold the ribbon off to one side as with other knots. Avoid pulling the stitch too tight; the knot should be loose and flowery.

40. Needle Weaving Bar Stitch

Work this stitch in rectangle shapes, loops, or curves. I use it for underwater projects to create texture and anemone shapes. I have also used it for flowers.

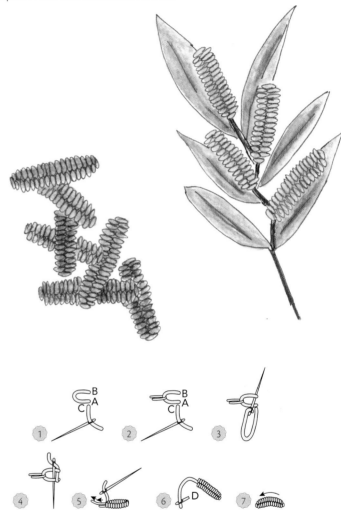

1 Come up at A. Form a loop and go down at B. Decide how wide the bar should be and make the loop that width. Come up just below A at C.

2 Pass a bobby pin, a paper clip, or a thread through the loop to hold the loop off the fabric.

3 Weave *over* the bottom thread and *under* the top thread.

4 Come back *over* the top thread and *under* the bottom. After each pass, push the woven thread snugly down to the previous wraps.

5 Once the loop is completely wrapped, remove the bobby pin, paper clip, or thread.

6–7 Make the bar curve by going into the fabric at D (just a bit shorter than the length of the bar).

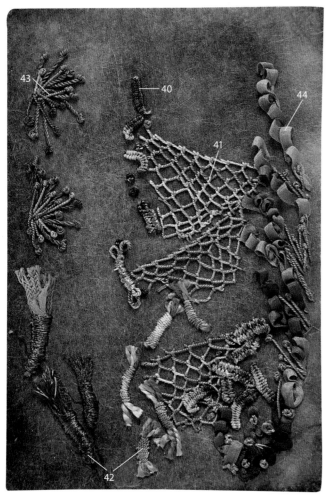

Stitches 40–44

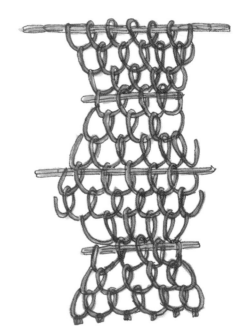

41. Net Stitch

Nothing says seaside more than the net stitch. Use it for fan corals, fishing nets, and background texture.

1   Make a row of stem stitches (page 57) to act as an anchor for the first row. Using a new thread, come up on the end of the stem stitch row at A. Holding down the thread, slide the needle under the first stem stitch, forming a loose buttonhole stitch (page 28). Make sure the needle lies over the loop.

2   Continue down the row.

3   Repeat this process for each row.

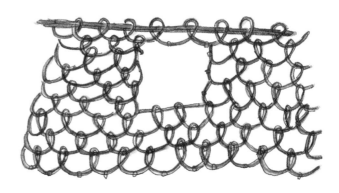

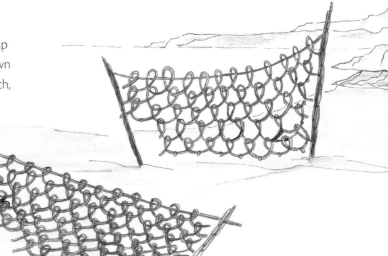

42. Overcast Stitch

I like to use this stitch to hold down loose threads. I wrap them by sewing the overcast stitch close together. It is wonderful for sea anemones and algae. Think texture with this stitch.

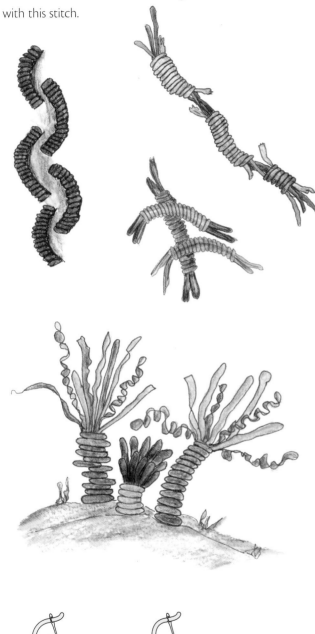

1–3 Mark a line the designated length of the overcast stitch. Cut threads to this length and place them on the marked line. Come up at A. Holding the cut threads on the marked line, go down at B and come up at C, working small satin stitches (page 53) with the wrapping thread. Keep the wraps close and even. When finished, take the ends of the cut threads to the back and secure.

43. Pistil Stitch

Used mostly for the centers of flowers, the pistil stitch can be elongated and distorted, depending on the choice of thread and yarn weight.

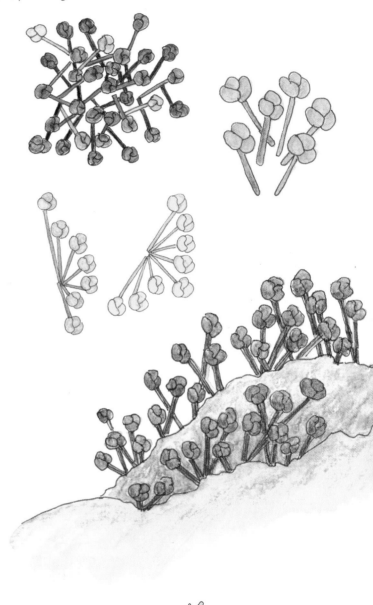

1 Come up at A, allowing a short length of thread, and wrap the working thread twice around the needle and form a French knot (page 40).

2–3 Go down at B (the length of the short thread plus the French knot), holding the knot in place until the needle is completely through the fabric.

44. Plume Stitch

This is a silk ribbon stitch that can be used for flowers, ferns, grasses, seaweed, and ground cover.

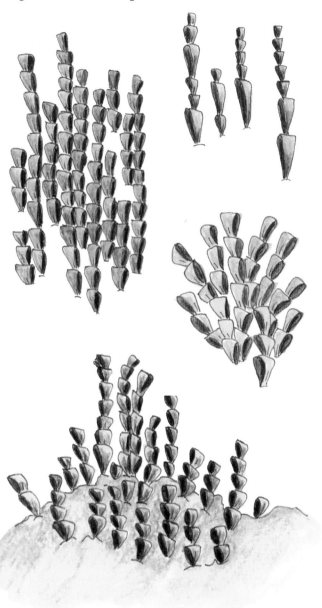

1. Come up at A and go down ⅛″ away at B to make a loop; control it with a round toothpick.

2–3. Hold the loop in place and come up at C, piercing both the fabric and the previous ribbon loop. Form another loop. Continue working downward until the plume is finished.

45. Raised Straight Stitch

Use the raised straight stitch in yarn to create flowers and underwater anemones. Vary the lengths of the stitches to create unusual shapes.

1. Mark the outer circle shape with dots. Mark a second smaller circle in the center. Divide the circle into quarters as shown. Come up on the center circle and go down on the outer circle.

2. Work the quarter-circle with straight stitches (page 57).

3–4. Complete the circle. Fill the center with French knots (page 40). Raise the straight stitches by running the needle under the stitches, gently pushing them up.

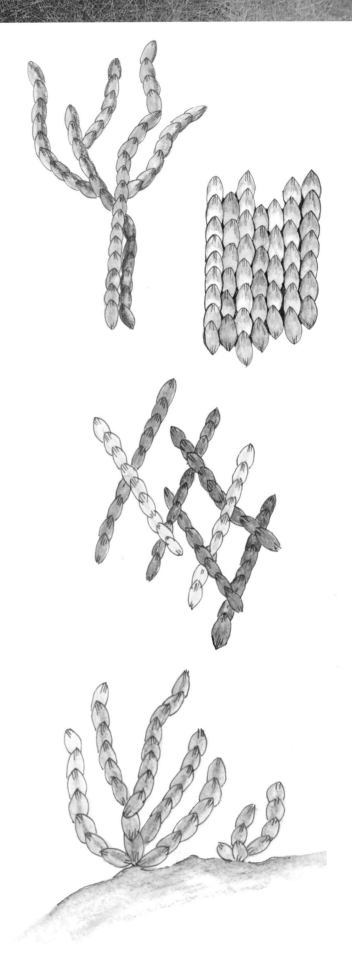

Stitches 45–49

46. Ribbon Split Stitch

I use this silk ribbon stitch often in landscapes and seascapes. It can be the trunks of trees, the stems of seaweed, and the walls or roofs of buildings. It fills in quickly.

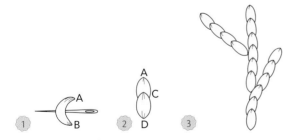

1. Come up at A and go down at B. Use the needle to keep the ribbon flat.

2. Come up in the center of the straight stitch at C, flatten the ribbon with the needle, and go back down at D.

3. Continue stitching for the desired length.

47. Romanian Couching

This stitch is wonderful for texture. It can be used in long shapes to create grasses and shrubs. It is particularly useful for filling in large spaces.

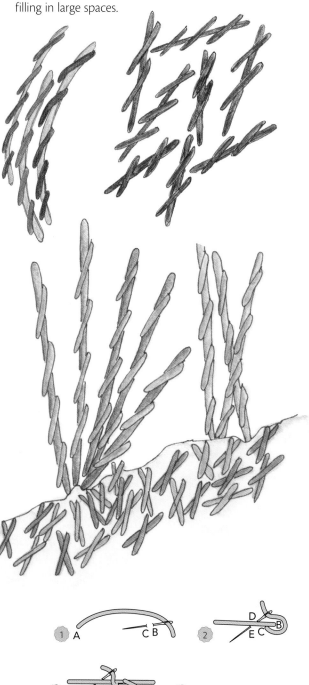

1   Bring the thread up at A. Carry it across the space to be filled. Go down at B and come up at C.

2   Bring the thread up and over the laid thread; then go down at D, and come up at E. This creates a diagonal couching stitch.

3–4   Continue down the laid thread at equal intervals.

48. Running Stitch

Use the straight stitch like a drawing line. If you vary the weight and length, the stitch can become lines of light on the ocean, lines on a cliff side, or grass and seaweed.

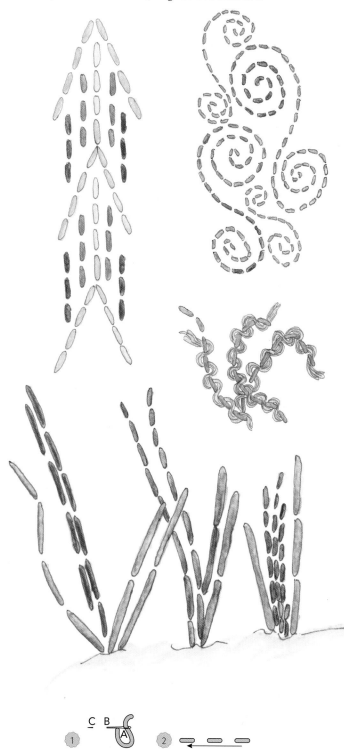

1–2   Come up at A, go down at B, and then up at C; continue making small, even stitches that are the same length as the spaces between them.

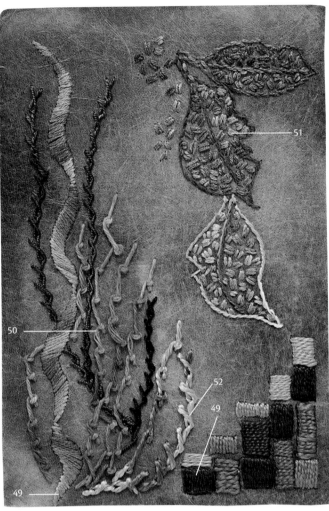

Stitches 49–52

49. Satin Stitch

This is a basic stitch that can be used for blocks of color to form hills, mountains, and valleys. Use it for floral and seaweed shapes as well.

1   Mark the shape as a guide for the stitches. Come up at A and go down at B, making a straight stitch (page 57) the desired length; then come up at C.

2–3   Continue working straight stitches close together, keeping the edge of the design even and defined. These stitches can be worked in single layers, or use double layers to create a thick, smooth blanket of stitching.

50. Scroll Stitch

This stitch works with everything from fine threads to heavy yarns and silk ribbons to create seaweed, grasses, and shrubs.

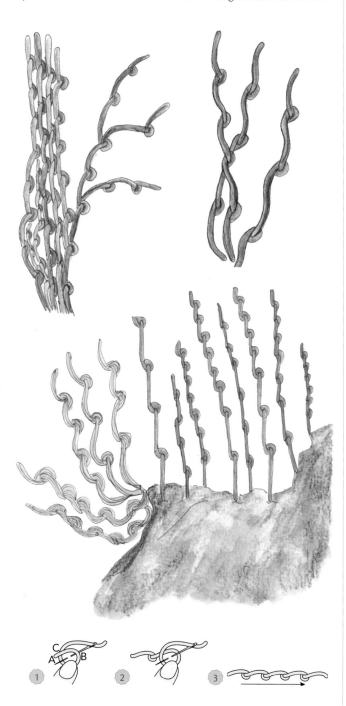

1–3 Come up at A. Loop the working thread to the right and hold it in place with your thumb. Go down at B and come up at C, making a small, slanted stitch in the center of the loop. Tighten the loop around the needle and pull the needle through. Continue, making a line of stitches.

51. Seed Stitch

Use these little stitches to create texture. I use them for texture on bark and leaves and seaweed.

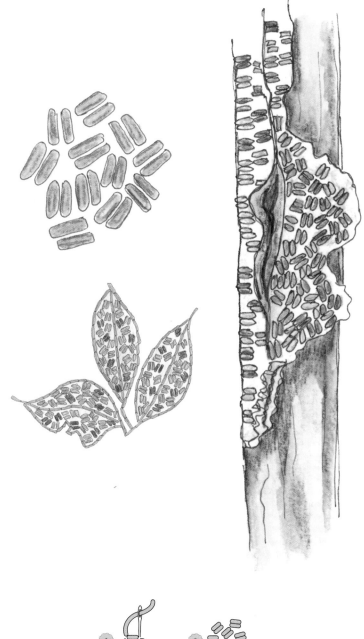

1–2 Come up at A and go down at B. Repeat for a second stitch, working the thread in the same holes, side by side.

Variation

Surround the seed stitches with an outline of backstitches (page 25) if you're creating leaves.

52. Snail Trail Stitch

Work the snail trail in chains to create floral and organic shapes. I use them in heavy yarn to create underwater anemones.

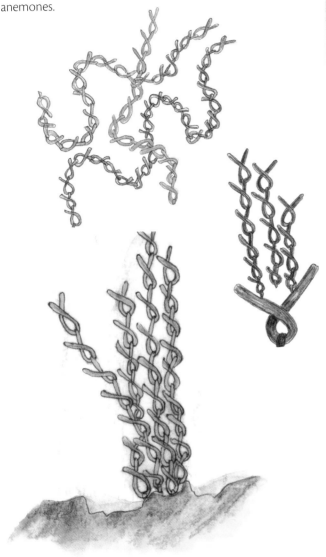

1–3 Work this stitch along a designated line. Come up at A, make a loop, and hold the thread with your thumb. Go down at B and then come up at C, bringing the needle tip over the thread. Vary the stitch by altering the stitch spacing and the slant of the needle.

53. Spider Web Backstitch

This is the stitch I use to create starfish and sea anemones. By changing the color and thread weight you can also create seashells.

1 Using a tapestry needle, stitch the spokes as shown (up at A, down at B, up at C, down at D, and so on), pulling each spoke firmly into place.

2 Make a small stitch in the center to hold down all the spokes.

3 Come up to the center top. Slide the needle under a spoke.

4 Continue working, easing back over 1 spoke and advancing under 2. Continue until the spokes are filled. Wrap the thread back around the final spoke.

Stitches 53–56

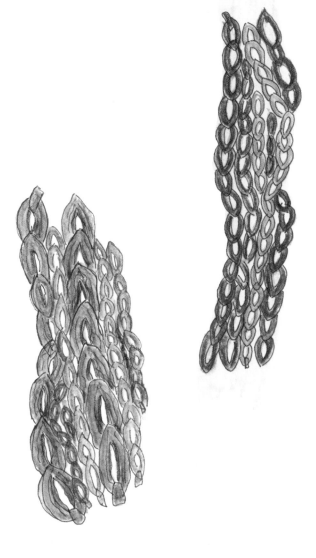

54. Split Stitch

This is a stitch best used with heavy yarns. Use it to create texture on tree trunks or sea plants.

1–2 Use a heavier thread (that you can split) for this stitch. Come up at A, make a small backstitch to B, and then come up at C, piercing the working thread in the middle.

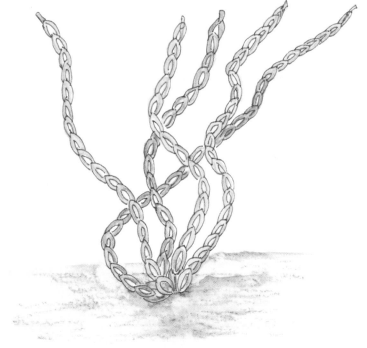

55. Stem Stitch

The stem stitch is also known as the outline stitch. Use it to create seaweed, grasses, and shrubs and to outline landscape shapes.

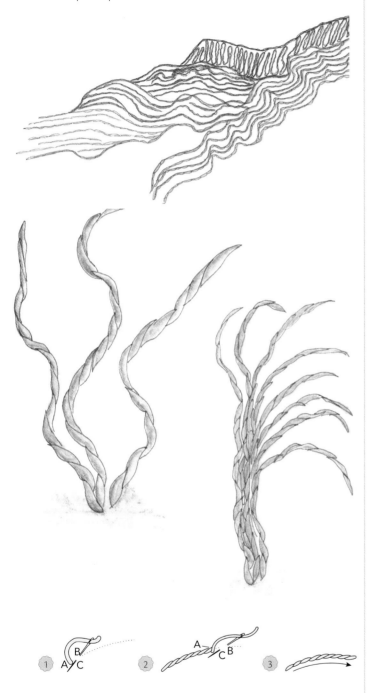

Note that for a straight line of stem stitches, the thread length will always be above the line (away from you). For a curved line of stem stitches, the thread length will be outside the curved line and the needle will always come up inside the curve (C).

1–3   Come up at A and go down at B in a short, slanting stitch. Come up at C (the midpoint of A and B). Repeat, keeping the stitches small and uniform.

56. Straight Stitch

Use the straight stitch for texture and line drawing. Think of it as a drawing line for crosshatching.

1–2   Come up at A and go down at B, pulling the thread firmly into place. Straight stitches can be worked evenly or irregularly and can vary in length and direction. Make them too loose or too long, however, and they could snag.

Stitches 14*, 57, and 58

57. String of Pearls Stitch

This is another line of knotted stitches that can form seaweed, shrubs, and tree branching. Vary the thread and yarn weights for more interest.

1   Come up at A. Hold the thread in a horizontal line with your left hand. Hold the needle perpendicular to the thread, take a small stitch down at B, and then come up at C. The tip of the needle lies over the thread; pull firmly into place.

2   Take the thread up under the bar to the right of the knot. Lay the thread in a small circle, surrounding the knot.

3–4   Go down just below the bar at D, close to the knot. Come up next to the knot at E; pull taut. Continue to the desired length of the stitch.

* For Twisted Chain Stitch, see 14. Chain Stitch: Twisted (page 32).

58. Van Dyke Stitch

Work this stitch upside down to create sea anemones and algae. Use heavy yarns and silk ribbons for heavier texture.

1 Work this stitch between 2 parallel lines. Come up at A, go down at B, and come up at C. Go down at D and come up at E.

2–3 Slide the needle under the crossed threads and gently pull the loop into place. The V formed at the top of the stitch should flare.

60

59 Detached

59 and
59 Detached

Stitches 59 and 60

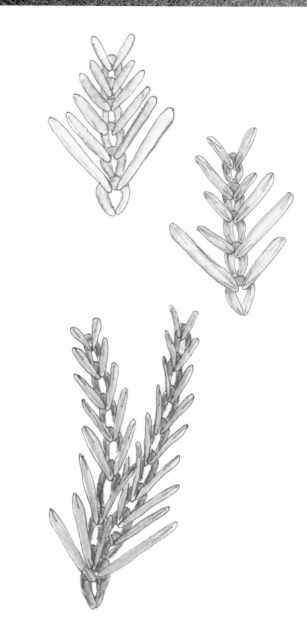

59. Wheat Ear Stitch and Wheat Ear Stitch: Detached

Use the wheat ear to create ferns and greenery. When using a single stitch it can become textural overlay, grasses, and shrub shapes.

1 Mark a line the desired length of the stitch. Come up at A and go down at B, slanting the stitch; then come up at C, even with and to the right of A. Go down again at D (as close to B as possible, but not into it) and come up at E.

2 Slide the needle under the slanted stitches to form a loop.

3–4 Go down again at F (as close to E as possible, but not into it) and come up at G, bringing the thread over the needle. Continue with the next stitch.

Wheat Ear Stitch: Detached

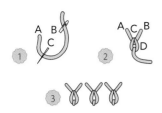

1 Come up at A. Go down at B and come back up at C. Keep the needle over the looped thread. Pull down and hold the thread with your free hand.

2–3 Make a second loop. Go down at C and come up at D. Anchor with a small stitch.

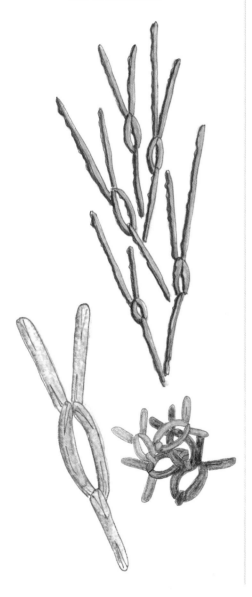

60. Whipstitch: Thread and Ribbon

Work the whipstitch in straight lines or curved shapes using heavy yarns, threads, or silk ribbon.

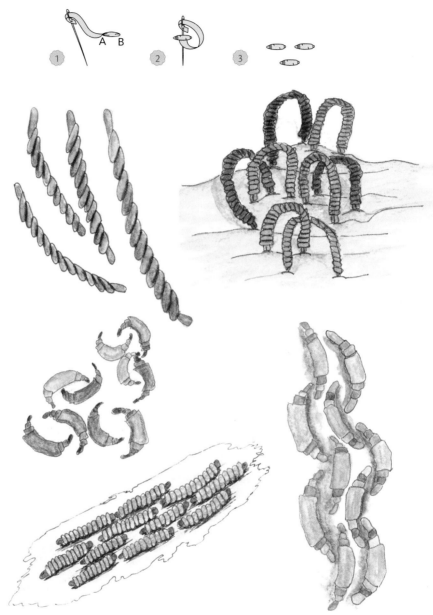

1 While keeping the ribbon flat, come up at A and go down at B, making a straight stitch (page 57) the desired length. Bring the needle up again at A.

2–3 Depending on the desired effect, wrap the straight stitch 2 or 3 times, keeping the ribbon flat. Anchor the stitch by passing the needle to the back.

Variation

Wrap the stitch, first working toward B and then working toward A to crowd the stitch so it will curve.

COMBINING STITCHES

Creating landscapes and seascapes with fabric, thread, and ribbon is a challenge that I enjoy. I use photographs, sketches, and watercolors to help me in the process. Drawing the lines and painting them in helps me "memorize" the overall design and layout.

Art Supplies

Note

Throughout this chapter, refer to the suggested stitches in the Stitch Guide (pages 23–61).

I keep various-sized Moleskine watercolor notebooks on hand. I purchase them from www.moleskine.com. I keep a pocket-sized watercolor Moleskine in my purse at all times, for fast sketches and notes. In the studio I keep a shelf of larger watercolor Moleskines. I use these for illustrations and watercolor projects that will serve as research for fiber art projects. I write notes and observations to myself right on the pages. This helps me remember the texture and feel of the tree trunks, the leaf canopy, or the grasses on the hill.

I work with Pigma Micron pens for the pen-and-ink lines, along with Derwent Inktense watercolor pencils and Winsor & Newton watercolor paints. I often use the Sakura Koi water brushes, which hold water in the handle and make for less mess.

Trees

The first section of this chapter is designed to help you choose tree trunk shapes and types of trees. For example, the Douglas fir is a Rocky Mountain evergreen, and it has certain characteristics. The twisted, gnarly Monterey cypress grows along the Western coastline with its own set of characteristics—you really need to know specific growth patterns and locations to create a believable landscape.

TREE TRUNKS

Tree trunks have a lot of character, and as they age the trunks become rougher and more scarred. The trunk is the main body—the core—and it holds the branches and tree canopy aloft. There are various ways to create fiber art trees, as you will see in the following suggestions.

TWISTED YARNS AND RIBBONS

1. Gather several yarns and ribbons that resemble the color and texture of the tree trunk.

2. Cut the yarns and ribbons twice as long as needed. Fold them in half—the fold will now form the bottom of the trunk.

3. Twist the yarns and ribbons loosely and tack in place. Separate some threads and ribbons toward the top for branches. Twist the branches and tack them in place.

4. Use embroidery threads or yarns to add more detail with running stitches, knots, or straight stitches. Add chain-stitch branches. Additionally, see the photo (page 66) for examples of tree trunks made from twisted yarns and ribbons.

SILK RIBBON STEM STITCH TRUNKS AND BRANCHES

1. Draw the outline of the tree on the actual project with a water-soluble pen.

2. Using 4mm silk ribbon, fill in the trunk with stem stitches in vertical rows. Make sure the edges of the ribbon gently overlap the previous row. Add the branches and twigs.

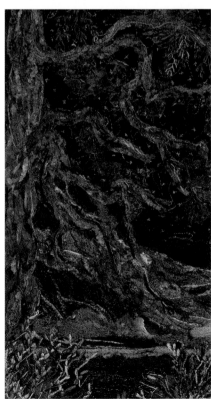

EMBROIDERED TREE TRUNKS AND BRANCHES

1. Draw the outline of the tree on the fabric.

2. Use the stem stitch along the outside lines. You can use several rows of stem stitch to create a shaded edge.

3. Use the chain stitch or the twisted chain to fill in. Be aware of the light and dark areas on the trunk and branches.

BURNED-EDGE TREE TRUNKS

1. Choose a cotton or silk fabric that best resembles the tree you want to create. Trace a pattern onto the fabric, making sure the lines run vertically. Cut the shape out a few threads beyond the line, as you will burn down to the pattern line.

2. Hold the fabric up to a steady candle flame. Slowly singe the edges (most fabrics will change color, creating a drawn line). Be sure to hold your hand steady. If the fabric flames, simply pinch the edge.

3. Tack the fabric trunk in place using running stitches. Then use various stitches such as chain stitch, satin stitch, and Romanian couching to create more detail and texture.

EMBELLISHED TWISTED TREE

1. Follow the directions under Twisted Yarns and Ribbons (page 64) to create the trunk.

2. Using an embellisher or needle-felting needle(s), very gently start punching the twisted yarns and ribbons into place. Go over them several times to create a smoother finish.

3. Split the yarns and ribbons toward the top to create branches.

This is a sampler of trees and shrubs. As you can see, the stitches are quite basic but very effective.

In the photo (above) the left tree trunk is made from fabric. The edges have been burned to give a more organic edge. The canopy is hand-dyed cheese-cloth and scrim, held in place with featherstitches and straight stitches.

Along the left side edge are small shrubs made with overlapping feather-stitches, French knots, and couched straight stitches.

The next trunk over is made with twisted yarns and ribbons. The twists are held in place with straight stitches. At the top is a small embroidered tree made with stem stitch, chain stitch, and featherstitch.

In the center is a rust-colored tree made with stem stitch and chain stitch, and the branches are made with chain stitch and featherstitch over hand-dyed cheesecloth.

To the right side is a twisted-yarn-and-ribbon trunk that has been felted with an embellisher.

Along the bottom are several shrubs and two small trees. One is hand-dyed lace shattered with scissors and tacked into place.

Don't be afraid to overlap stitches to create depth and texture. Everything from trees to shrubs has a background, midground, and foreground. In order to create this depth, you must run over previous stitches!

TREE TYPES

1. Aspen

Aspen trees grow in clonal colonies and spread by root suckers from a single parent tree. The trunks are creamy white with black and dark brown horizontal lines.

Trunk and bark: Use strips of dyed cotton or silk. Burn the edges with a candle to create a dark edge and the right shape. With embroidery threads, create markings on the trunk. Use the straight stitch, chain stitch, running stitch, and satin stitch.

Branch and leaf area: For leaf clusters, use hand-dyed cheesecloth or organza and cut into a general shape. Arrange in place and overlay with featherstitches or straight stitches. Make sure some of the chain-stitch branches are behind and on top of the cheesecloth to create depth.

Leaves: Cut shapes from hand-dyed organza for stylized and large leaves. Burn the edges to create a drawing line. Tack in place. To embroider aspen leaves, use the fishbone stitch, satin stitch, featherstitch leaf, arrowhead leaf stitch, and long and short stitch.

2. Birch

Birch trees are medium sized with white or silver-colored bark displaying horizontal lenticels or ridges. The bark peels into thin papery sheets.

Tree trunk and bark: Use chain stitches sewn side by side for the trunk and branches. Overlay these with seed stitches and overcast stitches; add in more detail with straight stitches.

Or use 4mm silk ribbon to make the trunk with the ribbon split stitch; place the ribbons in rows side by side to create a flat overlapping pattern.

Leaf canopy: Cut the general shape of leaf clusters from black netting. Use an embellisher (or hand needle-felting needles) to felt it in place to create shadows. Start with the finest threads to create the leaves, using the featherstitch and fly stitch. Overlay the stitches, moving from fine to heavier threads. Create twigs and branches with the chain stitch, coral stitch, straight stitch, and scroll stitch.

Leaves: For large leaves, use the stem stitch to outline the leaf shapes; fill in with seed stitches. You can also use the featherstitch leaf, fishbone leaf stitch, satin stitch, or stacked arrowhead stitch.

3. Cypress

The Monterey cypress is a medium-sized evergreen tree that often has a flat top and twisted limbs due to the high winds along the coast.

Trunk and branches: Gather several yarns, silk ribbons, and organza strips together.

Fold them in half with the fold at the bottom, twist, and then pin in the shape of the trunk. Tack the trunk in place with straight stitches or hold it in place using an embellisher (or hand needle-felting needles). Create texture with Romanian couching, twisted chain stitches, and chain stitches.

Or embroider the tree shape with chain stitches side by side; add texture using an embellisher (or hand needle-felting needles). Create knots and more texture with colonial knots, chain stitches, or twisted chain stitches.

Bark: The bark is rough and stringy, so use yarns or silk ribbon for stitching. Use the embellisher to rough them up.

Leaves: These are scalelike leaves. Form them using the fly stitch, fern leaf stitch, or wheat ear stitch; overlap them to create depth.

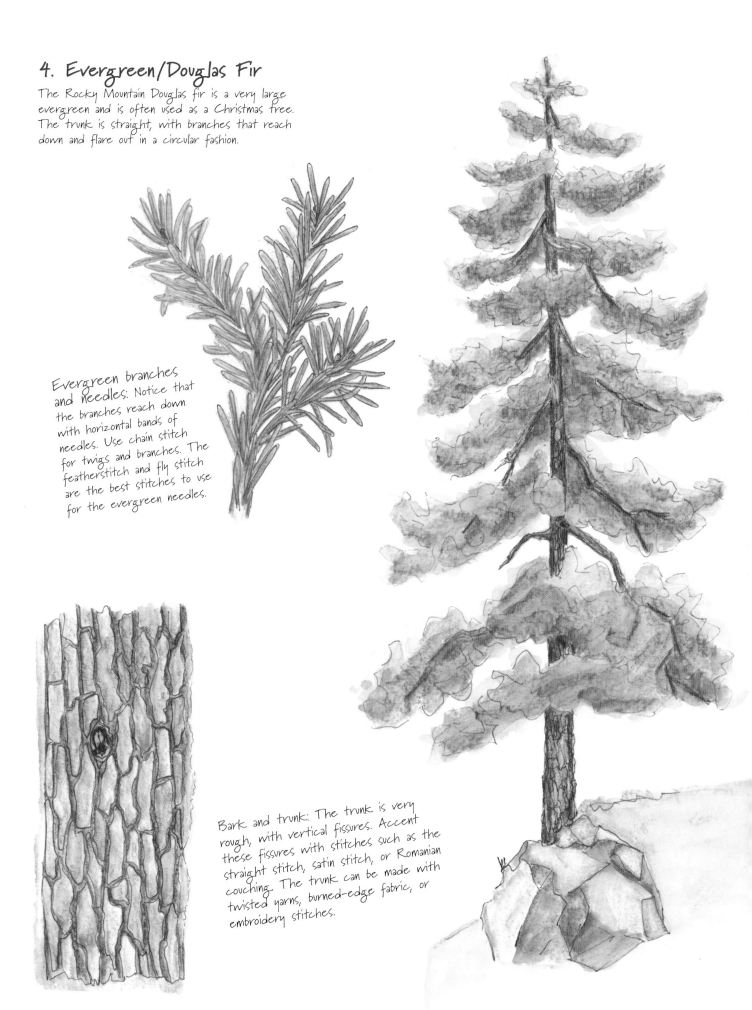

4. Evergreen/Douglas Fir

The Rocky Mountain Douglas fir is a very large evergreen and is often used as a Christmas tree. The trunk is straight, with branches that reach down and flare out in a circular fashion.

Evergreen branches and needles: Notice that the branches reach down with horizontal bands of needles. Use chain stitch for twigs and branches. The featherstitch and fly stitch are the best stitches to use for the evergreen needles.

Bark and trunk: The trunk is very rough, with vertical fissures. Accent these fissures with stitches such as the straight stitch, satin stitch, or Romanian couching. The trunk can be made with twisted yarns, burned-edge fabric, or embroidery stitches.

5. Gum Tree/Eucalyptus

Gum trees are associated with Australia but can be seen all over the world. They have tall, reaching branches with canopies of long, narrow evergreen leaves.

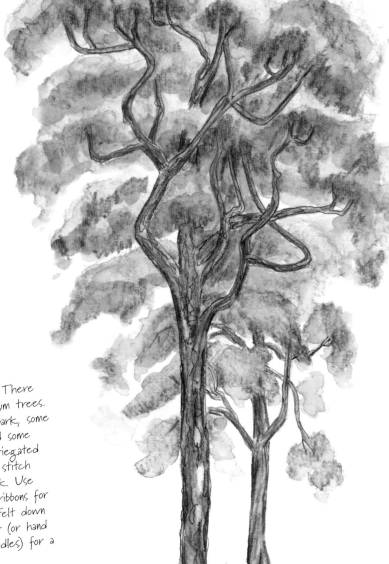

Leaf canopy and branches: The branches are sensuous lines and act like fingers to hold up the clusters of leaves. Use the chain stitch. Tack single layers of dyed cheesecloth in place to act as a background for featherstitch leaves.

Bark and trunk: There are many types of gum trees. Some have stringy bark, some have flaky bark, and some are smooth. Use variegated silk ribbon in a split stitch for the smooth bark. Use twisted yarns and ribbons for the other barks. Felt down with an embellisher (or hand needle-felting needles) for a smoother texture.

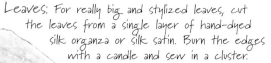

Leaves: For really big and stylized leaves, cut the leaves from a single layer of hand-dyed silk organza or silk satin. Burn the edges with a candle and sew in a cluster.

Embroider the leaves using the satin stitch, fishbone stitch, and stacked arrowhead stitch.

6. Juniper

Junipers are evergreens that often have rough, distorted trunks and branches. They are long-lived and able to withstand drought and cold. Juniper berries are used in cooking and give gin its special flavor.

Tree trunk and leaf canopy: The trunk is very rough, with wind-distorted branches and twigs. The needles can be made with straight stitches and featherstitches. Use worsted wool to embroider the trunk with twisted chain stitches and long and short stitches. Use the worsted wool for branches made with coral, scroll, or string of pearls stitches.

Needles: For close-up details, the overcast stitch and the bullion stitch make great evergreen needles. Otherwise, use the straight stitch, fern leaf stitch, fly stitch, and featherstitch. Notice that the needles cluster at the ends of the branches and grow in horizontal clumps.

Trunk detail: Use French knots and whipstitches to add detail to knot holes.

7. Maple

The maple tree is Canada's national tree, and a red maple leaf adorns the flag. The maple is a large deciduous tree that turns scarlet and orange in the crisp, cold fall. It also produces the sap from which maple syrup is made.

Trunk detail: Build up the trunk using yarns and rough threads. Use twisted chain and overlapping chain stitches to create deep fissures on older trunks

Tree trunk and canopy: The trunk is straight and branches out into a rounded form.

Block in the leaf placement with hand-dyed cheesecloth shapes. Overlap with chain-stitch branches and featherstitch twigs.

Leaves: The leaves have a very distinct shape with angular lines. Create them with satin stitches, stacked arrowhead stitches, and fly stitch leaves. Trace actual maple leaves onto hand-dyed organza. Cut out and burn the edges for more realistic shapes.

8. Oak

The mighty oak can be found throughout the world. It is a very large deciduous tree, producing acorns that provide food for many animals. It is a long-living tree with legendary qualities.

Leaf canopy: Use hand-dyed cheesecloth and scrim to create the background of the tree branches. Make sure some lies behind the branches and some lies on top. This creates more depth. Use the chain stitch and stem stitch to create twigs and branches.

Tree trunk and canopy: Oak trees become very rough and gnarly as they age, with deep fissures. Over time the bark turns gray, with moss and lichen adding to the color.

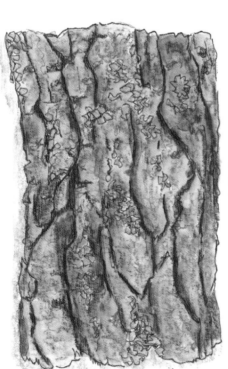

Trunk detail: Create the bark with embroidery yarns using the chain stitch, twisted chain stitch, and stem stitch. Use an embellisher (or hand needle-felting needles) to smooth down the stitches. Add the moss and lichen with French knots, seed stitches, and Judith's knotted flower stitches. Twisted yarns and silk ribbons make wonderful trunks and bark.

After embellishing the materials, add more chain stitches and twisted chain stitches for texture.

Leaves: Use the satin stitch, stem stitch, fishbone stitch, and flat stitch to make oak leaves. Oak leaves turn deep red in the fall.

9. Palm

Palm trees have very tall, singular trunks with a topknot of evergreen leaf fronds. They are warm-weather trees that grow from the tropics to the desert. Some palm trees produce coconuts or dates. Palm leaves are often used for basketry, clothing, and food preparation.

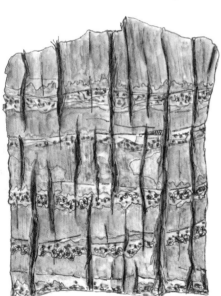

Bark details: There are horizontal growth bands with deep vertical fissures. Use straight stitches and stem stitches to create a crisscross effect.

Leaves: The Van Dyke stitch and the wheat ear stitch make great palm leaf fronds. Make sure there is a definite spine separating the individual leaves.

Tree trunk and top: Create the trunk with 4mm silk ribbon and the stem stitch.

Add the growth rings with horizontal stem stitch or rows of French knots. The palm leaves can be created with the fly stitch leaf, fern leaf stitch, and leaf ribbon stitch.

10. Willow

The willow tree is large and is defined by long, slender weeping branches weighed down with hanging narrow leaves. It is used in the production of aspirin and charcoal. The bark is rough and gray, marked by long, branching ridges that result in deep furrows. The twigs are rust and light green.

Leaves: Cut the leaf shapes from hand-dyed silk ribbon for larger, stylized leaves. Burn the edges to create a more realistic look. Use the satin stitch, fishbone stitch, and stacked arrowhead stitch for embroidered leaves.

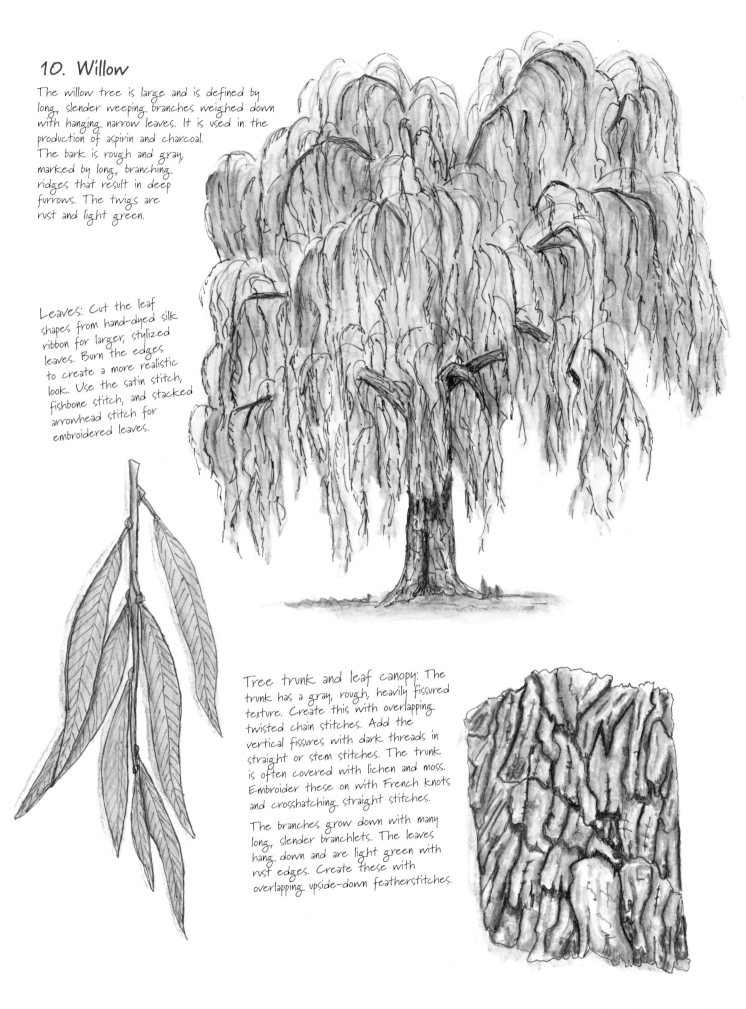

Tree trunk and leaf canopy: The trunk has a gray, rough, heavily fissured texture. Create this with overlapping twisted chain stitches. Add the vertical fissures with dark threads in straight or stem stitches. The trunk is often covered with lichen and moss. Embroider these on with French knots and crosshatching straight stitches.

The branches grow down with many long, slender branchlets. The leaves hang down and are light green with rust edges. Create these with overlapping upside-down featherstitches.

TREE SHAPES

Umbrella (flowering dogwood)

Upright oval (red maple)

Vase (goldenrain)

Round
(Ohio buckeye)

It is good to know the general shapes of different trees. The background shape can be cut out of organza, cheesecloth, or scrim. The embroidery stitches are worked on top.

Pay special attention to the way tree branches grow. Are they upright, horizontal, or growing downward? Use stem stitch, chain stitch, coral stitch, and straight stitch for the branches. Make sure the branches show through the leaf canopy.

Horizontal oval (hawthorn)

Broad triangle (pine oak)

Mound (Tamukeyama)

Narrow triangle (Austrian pine)

Narrow upright (northern catalpa)

Weeping (weeping cherry)

Palm (Indian date palm)

Columnar (Leyland cypress)

Pay attention to the size of trees. Are they extra large or short and squat? Do they grow in clusters or as lone sentinels? Create shadows by using light and dark shades of the chosen thread color. Trees also cast shadows on the ground or surrounding shrubbery.

Shrubs

Shrubs come in all sizes, from ground-hugging junipers to tall, open sumac. They add texture and depth to any landscape.

Always study the landscape to view the patterns of the trees and shrubbery. Note whether the shrubs cluster together or whether they form layers in the midground or foreground.

Be aware that the taller shrubs in the background have less detail. Use very simple embroidery lines such as fine-threaded running stitches. Suggest the detail with tiny featherstitches.

In the foreground use an embellisher (or hand needle-felting needles) to tack organza and tulle shrub shapes in place. This will allow the fabric to ruffle up, creating even more depth and texture. Work the free-form stitches into the ruffled layer. Continue working forward, making sure the stitches are larger and looser.

I keep files filled with drawings, photographs, magazine clippings, and sketches for research. I have everything from flowers to clouds in the files—I even have one for shrubs. It is hard to remember what shrub goes with what regional hillside, so make notes!

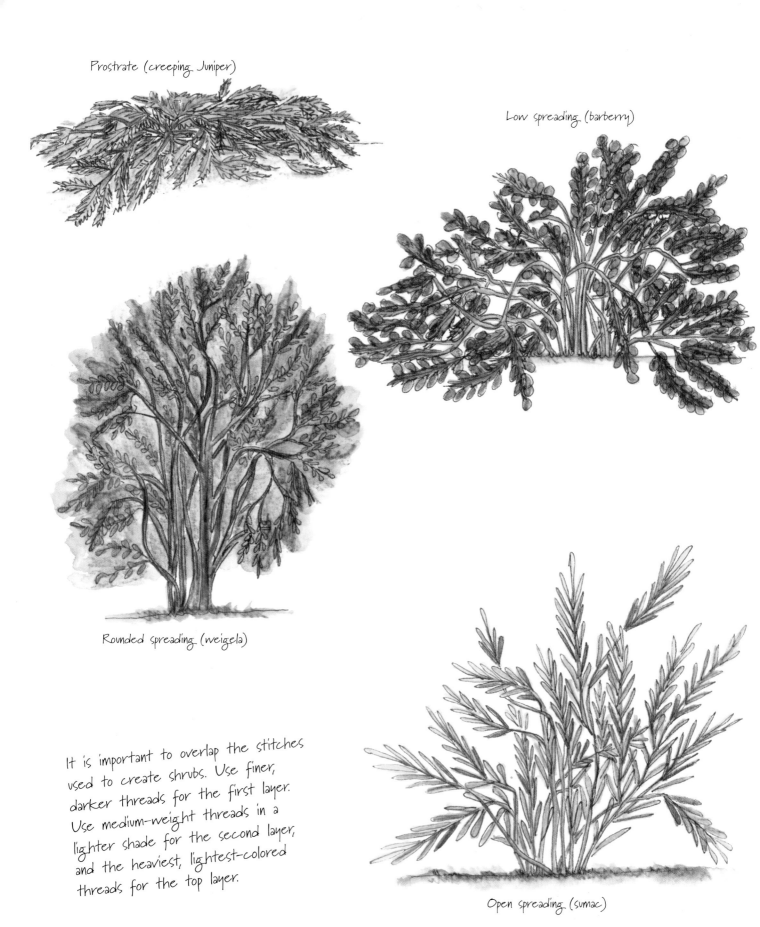

Prostrate (creeping Juniper)

Low spreading (barberry)

Rounded spreading (weigela)

It is important to overlap the stitches used to create shrubs. Use finer, darker threads for the first layer. Use medium-weight threads in a lighter shade for the second layer, and the heaviest, lightest-colored threads for the top layer.

Open spreading (sumac)

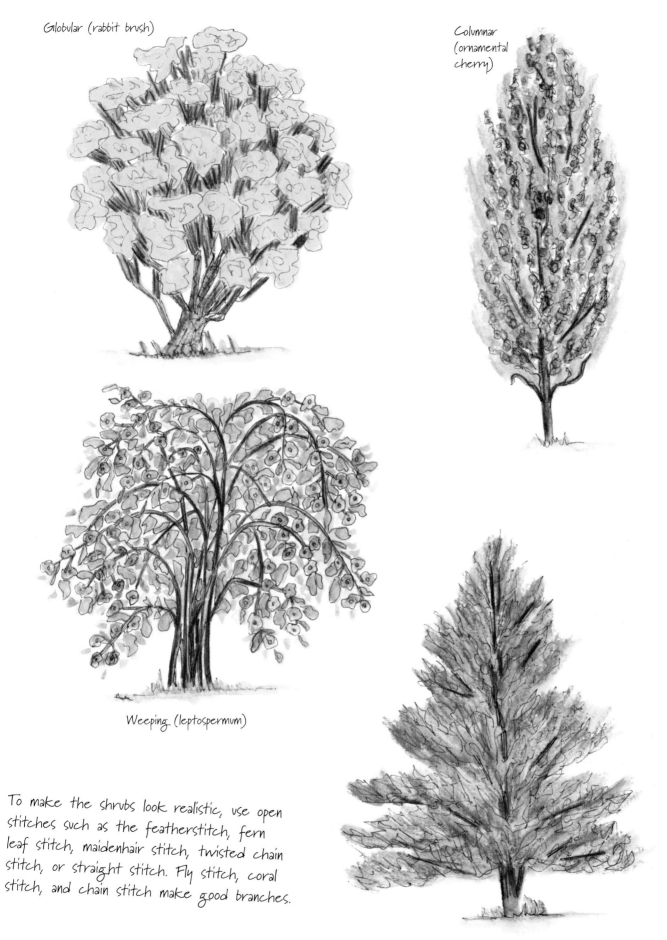

Globular (rabbit brush)

Columnar
(ornamental
cherry)

Weeping (leptospermum)

To make the shrubs look realistic, use open
stitches such as the featherstitch, fern
leaf stitch, maidenhair stitch, twisted chain
stitch, or straight stitch. Fly stitch, coral
stitch, and chain stitch make good branches.

Pyramidal (nigra evergreen)

Vines

Vines are defined as weak-stemmed plants that derive support from climbing, twining, or creeping along a surface.

There is an evil beauty to many vines (such as kudzu) because they flower with gay abandon, all the while choking the life from their host. Many vines twine around tree trunks and peek out of treetops, while some cling to the sides of buildings and slide over stone walls. Some vines are grown for their beautiful flowers (clematis, potato vine), while others are grown for their fruit (grapes, passion fruit).

Vines are fun to create with embroidery stitches, and they add another layer of texture. Use the chain stitch and the stem stitch to create the main body of the vine. The threaded backstitch will also make a realistic vine, as several threads will be used in the process. Choose from the many floral stitches to create the beautiful vine flowers.

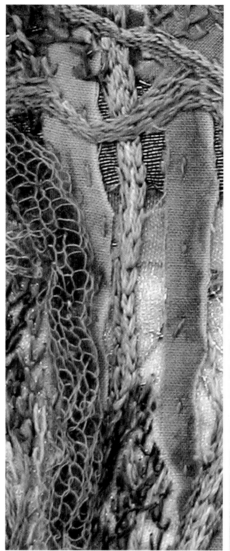

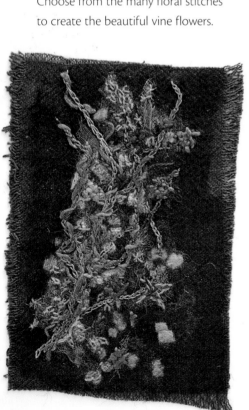

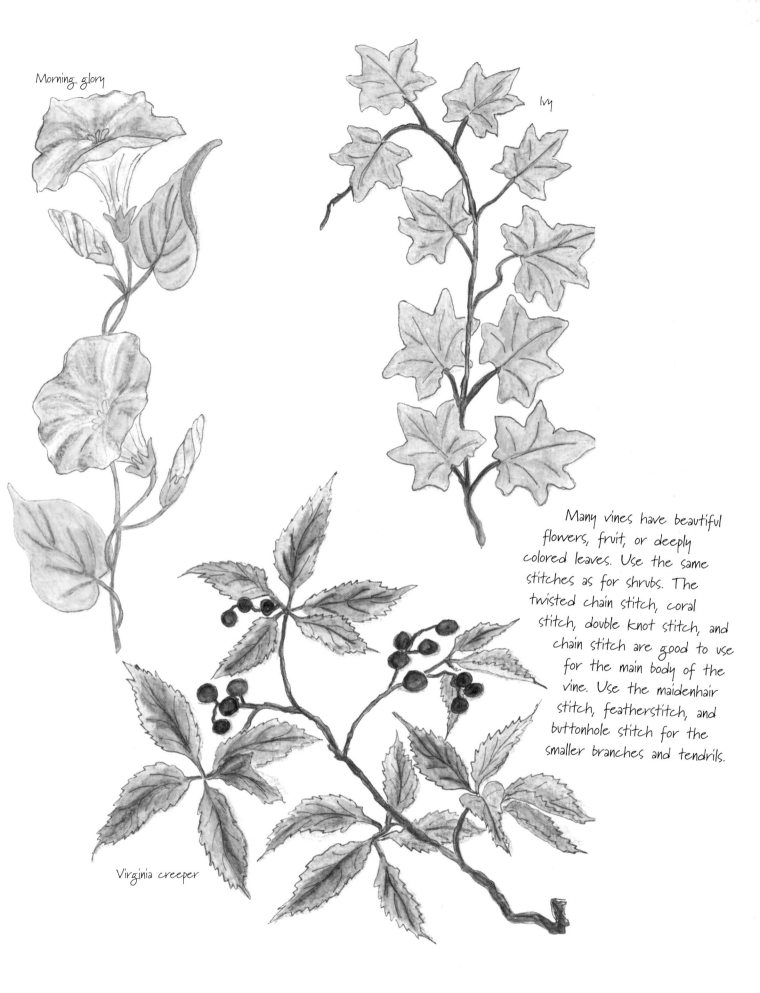

Morning glory

Ivy

Virginia creeper

Many vines have beautiful flowers, fruit, or deeply colored leaves. Use the same stitches as for shrubs. The twisted chain stitch, coral stitch, double knot stitch, and chain stitch are good to use for the main body of the vine. Use the maidenhair stitch, featherstitch, and buttonhole stitch for the smaller branches and tendrils.

Use the stem stitch and chain stitch to create the undulating vine shapes. The threaded backstitch is good for creating more texture. The coral stitch, string of pearls stitch, couched threads, double knot stitch, scroll stitch, and maidenhair stitch can create vines of all types and shapes. Add flower or fruit shapes with French knots, lazy daisy stitches, and colonial knots.

Wisteria

Climbing rose

Creeping fig

Grasses and Weeds

Many landscapes feature layers of waving grassy fields and clusters of weeds. Depending on the season, the grasses add color and texture to a landscape.

Be aware that grass and weeds cannot be seen way off in the background, and in the midground there will be just a hint of them. Use very fine threads for the midground, creating layers of straight stitch and fly stitch.

Highlight the grasses in the foreground with seedpods and the odd flowering head sticking up above the rest. Use heavier, more colorful threads toward the front.

Weeds always stand out from the surrounding grasses. As a gardener, I know they are stronger and manage to take up more nutrients and water than their neighbors. So it stands to reason that they either grow taller and bigger or they creep along and choke out a patch of good stuff!

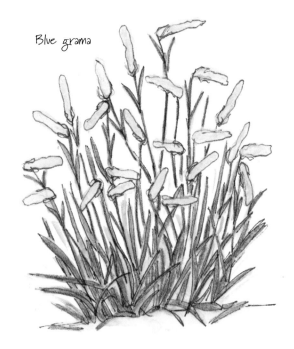

Blue grama

To create grass shapes, use fine threads in long, loose overlapping stitches such as lazy daisy, straight stitch, couched straight stitch, elongated buttonhole stitch, coral stitch, and pistil stitch. Use colonial knots, braid stitches, fly stitch seedpods, and head of the bull stitches for seed or grain heads.

Giant sacaton

Indian grass

Seagrass

Some grasses are thin and wispy at the end of each blade. To create this look, combine two stitches, such as a chain-stitch base with a long sweep of stem stitch toward the top. Use an elongated lazy daisy stitch with an extra-long catch stitch.

Many grasses are faded or dried out at the tips. Create this look with variegated threads.

Little bluestem

Desert grass

Dandelion heads can be made with the fly stitch seedpods, and thistle heads can be made from overlapping head of the bull stitches. The prickles on stems and leaves are made with small straight stitches.

Use colonial knots for many flowering weeds. Use satin stitches for the leaves on dandelions and thistles.

Dandelion

Thistle

Tumbleweeds are a jumble of overlapping featherstitches and maidenhair stitches. The finer threads are used in the back. Use three shades of one color to create depth.

Tumbleweed

Underwater Shapes and Corals

There is another world under the sea, and I am totally in love with it. The differences between underwater scenes and landscapes and seascapes are the light source, terrain, and wildlife.

The light source for underwater scenes comes from above, creating shafts of light from the top down. There are valleys, hills, cliffs, and caves under the water. The wildlife includes various types of fish, anemones, corals, and even mammals.

Once you know how to create trees, shrubs, grasses, and vines, you will have no problem creating underwater shapes. Vine shapes will become undulating kelp and seaweed. Grasses will become sea fans, corals, and algae. Flower head shapes become starfish, seashells, and button anemones.

Just remember that there is a background, midground, and foreground in an underwater scene. The background is created with layers of tulle and organza, much like the sky in a landscape or seascape. Start from the back and work forward, carefully creating the background, midground, and foreground sections.

The colors under the sea are much brighter and more intense, allowing for lots of thread and ribbon choices. This is the place for those slubby yarns, iridescent threads, and metallics. Underwater scenes also allow for a lot more surface work such as crochet stitches, twisted ribbons, and couched materials.

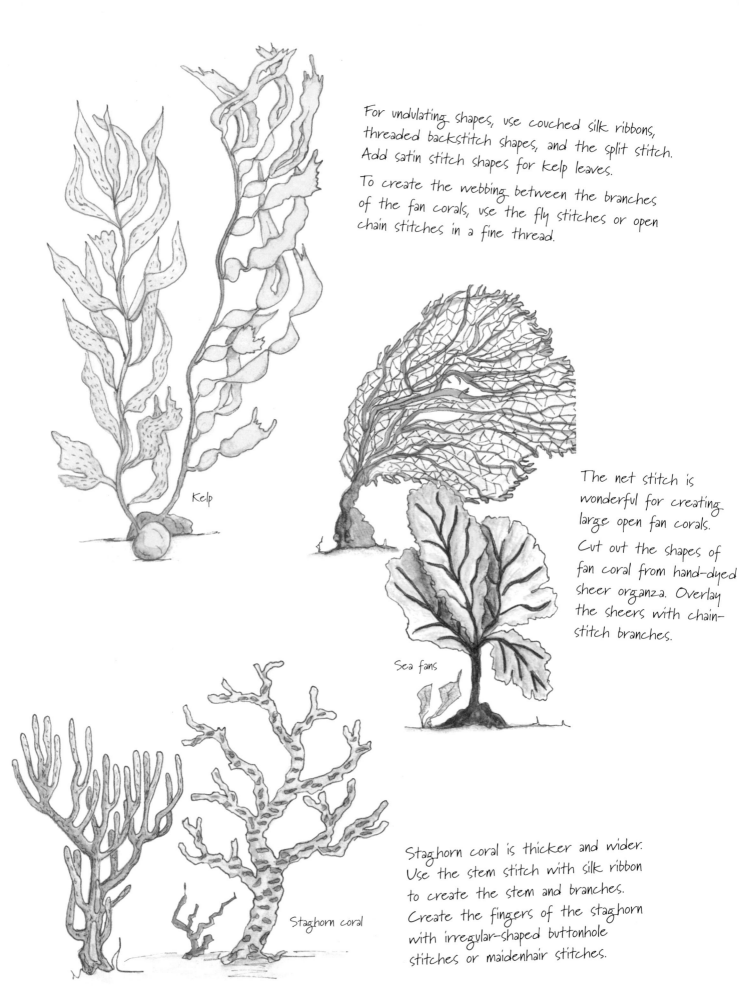

For undulating shapes, use couched silk ribbons, threaded backstitch shapes, and the split stitch. Add satin stitch shapes for kelp leaves.

To create the webbing between the branches of the fan corals, use the fly stitches or open chain stitches in a fine thread.

Kelp

The net stitch is wonderful for creating large open fan corals.

Cut out the shapes of fan coral from hand-dyed sheer organza. Overlay the sheers with chain-stitch branches.

Sea fans

Staghorn coral

Staghorn coral is thicker and wider. Use the stem stitch with silk ribbon to create the stem and branches. Create the fingers of the staghorn with irregular-shaped buttonhole stitches or maidenhair stitches.

Algae are those little colorful wavy bits that cling to rocks in the ocean rock pools. They come in all shapes, colors, and sizes. Use silk ribbon plume stitches, overcast stitches, knotted buttonhole stitches, Judith's knotted flower stitches, and silk ribbon loop stitches to create various algae shapes. For the larger feathery algae shapes, use satin stitches and fishbone stitches.

Algae

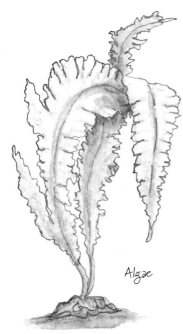

Algae

Brain corals are either oval or round shapes with deep fissures. Use tight circular buttonhole stitches for the basic shapes. For larger brain corals, cut out the basic shapes from hand-dyed silk velvet. Create the ridges with side-by-side French knots.

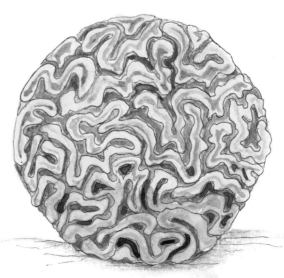

Brain coral

Button corals cling to rocks. They are very colorful when open but close up when alarmed. Use circular buttonhole stitches to create small circular shapes. Cluster them side by side. Use the eyelet stitch to create circular shapes. Montano knots and colonial knots will work well when clustered together. Use 4mm silk ribbon and heavier threads for more texture.

Button coral

Sea anemones are fun to create. With long and short stitches, create the bulblike body. Use stem stitches to create the tentacles. The overcast stitch creates wonderful anemones. Use colorful threads and yarns bunched together and wrap them with variegated thread to form the tubular body. Let the bundled threads hang out the top.

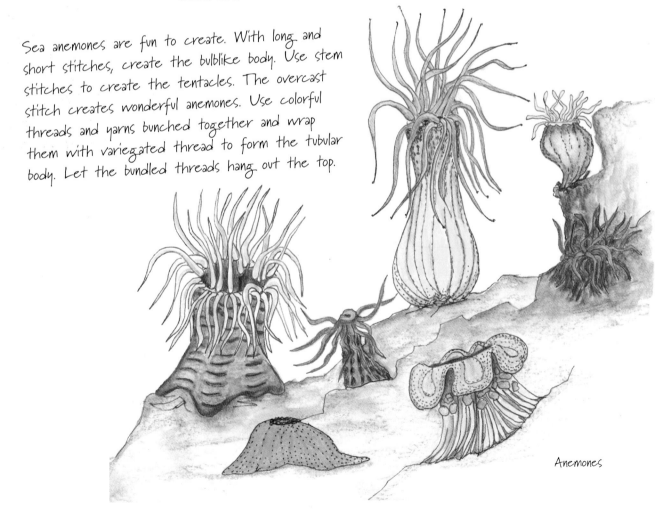

Anemones

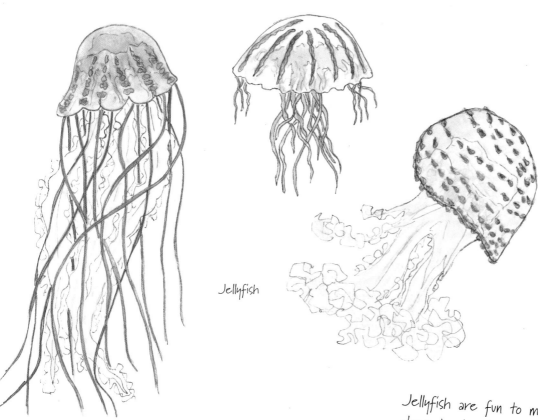

Jellyfish

Raised straight stitches and spider web backstitches are perfect for starfish shapes. Make them in bright, colorful threads. For smaller starfish shapes, use the arrowhead stitch and the backstitch star. Enjoy the process!

Jellyfish are fun to make. They are like upside-down bowls with long, floating tentacles. Create the tentacles first by couching down long straight stitches. Create the bowl shape with satin stitches or half-circle buttonhole stitches. To make fuller-looking tentacles, gather together several six-stranded threads. Fold them in half and tie them in the center with a loose knot. Let the threads hang down and then separate all the threads. Couch the threads in place. Cover the knot at the top with a half-circle of silk organza.

Starfish

Botanical Flower Shapes

Everyone enjoys flowers, and needle artists enjoy creating them. For me, adding floral shapes is like adding the icing to the cake. Floral shapes appear in landscapes, seascapes, and underwater scenes. They usually appear in the foreground to add more interest, texture, and depth.

Before starting your project, do some research on the plants and flowers of the region. I use Google search and I always look through the available photographs for more details.

Remember that you are painting with threads, yarns, and ribbons. Flowers will create blocks of color in the background and midground. Use simple stitches such as single-wrap French knots, running stitches, and straight stitches. The hint of flowers out in the field is better than overworked detail.

You can go for the detail in the foreground with floral shapes. Just remember again that you must overlap layers of stitching to create depth in the foreground. Don't be afraid to build up the stitches by overlaying previous stitches. Some of them will show through!

Please look through my embroidery book *Floral Stitches* for a concise stitch guide on floral shapes.

Use the stem stitch and chain stitch for creating stems. The chain stitch, fishbone stitch, and flat stitch are great for leaves. Be sure to use variegates and shades of solid colors for a more realistic look.

Use the loop stitch with silk ribbon for large petals. The satin stitch gives a smooth finish to the petals of most flowers. Use the raised straight stitch for daisy-type flowers.

Cup shape (tulip)

There are many different categorized shapes for flowers.

Cruciform (wallflower)

Star shape (star-of-Bethlehem)

Saucer shape (anemone)

Bell shape (English bluebells)

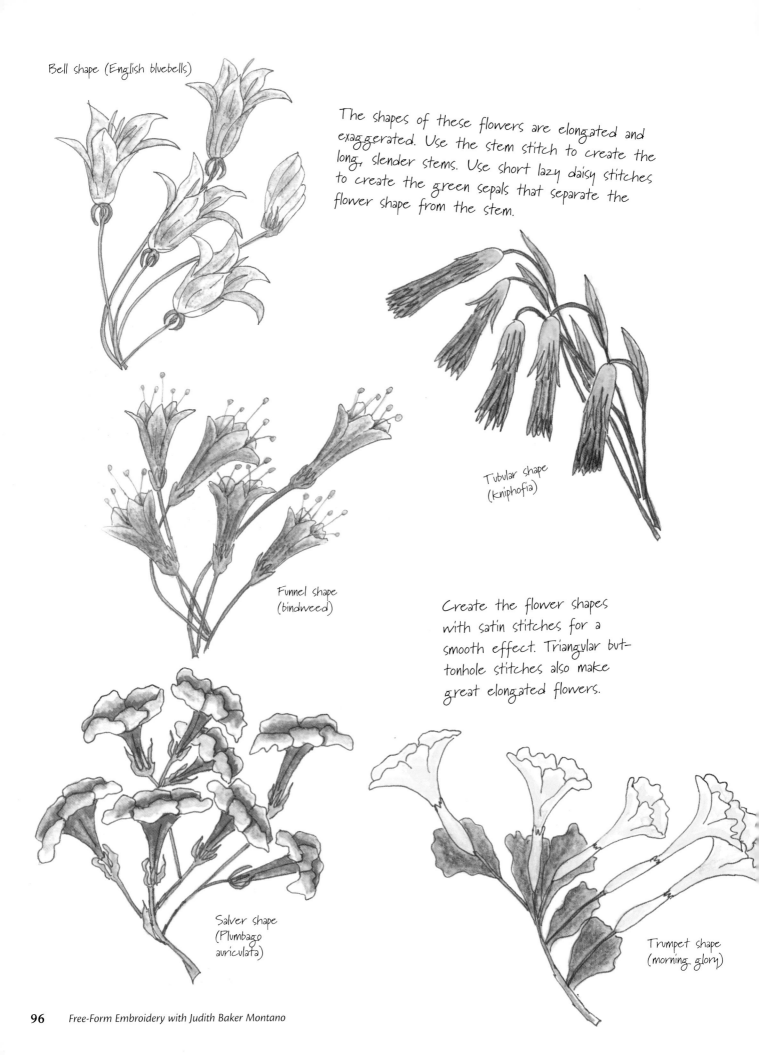

The shapes of these flowers are elongated and exaggerated. Use the stem stitch to create the long, slender stems. Use short lazy daisy stitches to create the green sepals that separate the flower shape from the stem.

Tubular shape (kniphofia)

Funnel shape (bindweed)

Create the flower shapes with satin stitches for a smooth effect. Triangular buttonhole stitches also make great elongated flowers.

Salver shape (Plumbago auriculata)

Trumpet shape (morning glory)

Rosette shape (dandelion)

Pom-pom shape
(bachelor's button)

For pom-pom and rosette-shaped flowers, use the circular buttonhole stitch or clustered French and colonial knots. Eyelet and raised straight stitches will work too.

Remember that each variety of flowers has different-colored green leaves and stems.

Pitcher shape
(sidesaddle flower)

For the pitcher- and slipper-shaped flowers, use satin stitches, chain stitches, and long and short stitches. Use variegates to create shading in the petals.

Slipper shape (slipperwort)

THINK LIKE A PAINTER

I love working with mixed media for my art projects. Each project is an adventure and a challenge, and I always learn something. Over the years I've become more confident with my embroidery stitches, to the point that I am constantly pushing the stitches into free-form shapes. So now I paint with the stitches, creating depth and texture. Thanks to mixed media, each project is a challenging adventure along with lots of mistakes and successes. It keeps me looking for the next project, or, as I call it , "The Great What If?"

South West Windows, 9″ × 6″, **Private Collection**

Ravens can be seen throughout the Southwest, and I never tire of watching them. The red rock formations of Sedona, Arizona, are breathtakingly beautiful and the ravens are numerous.

Materials: The raven sketch is ironed to hand-dyed silk using TAP, Transfer Artist Paper. The red rock formations are stitched using the buttonhole stitch, chain stitch, and long and short stitch. The windows are formed with overlapping 7mm silk ribbon and rayon ribbon. The embroidery stitches for the window sections are buttonhole stitch, running stitch, and decorated herringbone stitch.

From small free-form stitching projects to large landscapes, seascapes, and underwater scenes, mixing media gives me artistic license to use the many needlework techniques I've learned over the years. Now I have added painting, photography, computer skills, and felting. I continue to try different techniques and to experiment.

Stitching continues to be a special love. The challenge of pushing the traditional stitches into free-form shapes is addictive, and I am always anxious to get to the stitching part of my projects. I can draw with free-form stitches. If I don't like the effect of certain embroidery stitches, I can stitch right over them with other threads or ribbon. Hours will fly by when I am stitching!

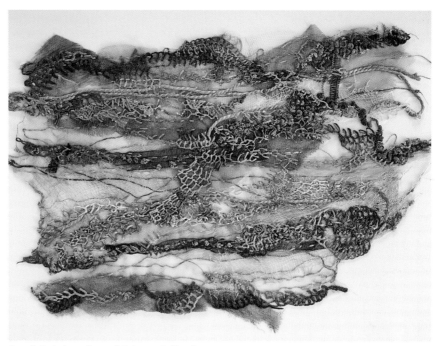

Beach Debris, 10″× 7½″, Private Collection

I love to walk along the beach looking for treasures. Beach debris drifts up in the seaweed that has washed ashore and holds shells, beach glass, driftwood, and many types of algae.

Materials: *Beach Debris* is a study of stitches worked over strips of hand-dyed silk organza and cheesecloth. The fabrics were wedged between two sheets of water-soluble material (which is rinsed away when the stitching is complete). The stitches that are worked over the fabrics, holding them in place, include buttonhole stitches, net stitches, running stitches, couched threads, French knots, and colonial knots.

River Rain Drops, 10″ × 7″, Private Collection

Looking down from our local bridge I can see all types of things floating on the surface of the water. Fallen leaves, twigs, and branches float serenely in the crystal-clear water. River rocks add shadows to the water, and the overhead trees add even more design.

Materials: Hand-dyed silk organza, silk ribbons, cheesecloth, and Hanah Silk ribbons form the background. Overlapping fabrics are sandwiched between two pieces of water-soluble material (which is rinsed away when the stitching is complete). The metallic threads are worked in running stitch and featherstitch. A sequined chainette ribbon is couched in place, and the chain stitch is used to outline the rectangle and square shapes.

From Paint to Fabric

My landscapes have evolved over many years. I started out as a child with pen and ink drawings and then became a painter of realistic landscapes. In university I created abstracts and impressionist landscapes and later made appliquéd wallhangings and quilts. While honing my quilting and crazy-quilt skills, I became interested in creating fabric landscapes and seascapes. After many years of trial and error, I realized that all the rules of painting applied to creating textile landscapes and seascapes.

The transition from paint to fabric is difficult, but it will be easier if you learn to think like a painter. Your canvas is now fabric. Paint has been replaced by fabrics, ribbons, threads, and yarns, which will be layered like a painter applies layers of paint. You have learned various crafts and needlework techniques over the years, and now you can combine them to create a unique work of art.

The rules of painting are simple, and they apply to photography, needlework, wearable art, and many other art forms. Read through the following rules before starting your project.

What Time of Day Is It?

Look for the light source at different times of the day. Early-morning light casts long shadows. As the sun rises in the sky, the shadows become shorter. At high noon there is no shadow, just flat light. Shadows increase with the afternoon light.

Detail from *Sand Dunes and Night Skies* (next page)

Where Is the Light Source?

All light sources will create shadows. The light source can be the sun, a campfire, a fireplace, a lamp, or neon lights on a busy street.

Where Do the Shadows Fall?

Shadows fall on the side away from the light source. If the light source is on the left side of an object, the shadow will be on the right. I use black netting or tulle to create shadows.

What Is the Weather?

A rainy day will be grayed, with soft shadows; a sunny beach will have light colors with deep shadows. A sunrise or sunset will use vibrant colors and dramatic shadows.

What Area of the Country Is This?

Intensity of light and color is determined by climate and country. Jungle greens will differ from the dusty greens of a desert. Skies are different colors depending on the location.

The Importance of the Horizon

The horizon divides the sky from the ground or sea. Do not place the horizon in the center of an artwork, as it is disturbing to the eye. Place the horizon line above or below the center of the landscape or seascape. The higher the horizontal line, the more midground and foreground there are for detailed needlework. A lower horizon line means there is less of a foreground for detail work.

Sand Dunes and Night Skies, 11″ × 15″, Private Collection

The Great Sand Dunes National Park and Preserve is one hour from my home in southern Colorado. These dunes of pure golden sand cover an area about 7 miles by 5 miles and are the tallest dunes in North America. The Sahara-like sand dunes against the base of the mountains make for wonderful photographs. A nearby ancient juniper, along with the star-filled Colorado night skies, influenced this project.

Materials: I used hand-dyed silk velvets and silk satin, organza, silk noil, sparkle netting, wool yarns, metallic threads, and Montano Series silk threads and ribbons. The tree is created with twisted felted silk strips and embroidery stitches. The stars and foreground shrubbery are embroidery stitches along with silk ribbon embroidery.

Three Elements of a Painting

Background

The background is the farthest point back in the painting. Everything in this area is small and far away. First arrange the sky fabric and then very small background pieces to give a feeling of distance. Detail cannot be seen in this area. Use very fine threads and tiny stitches to indicate size and distance.

Midground

Everything here is of medium proportions. It is the divider between "way back there" and "right here"! Things in the midground will be larger than things in the background. Everything in the midground is more visible, so work with medium-size threads and textural stitches. Some of these stitches will lie over the background stitching.

Foreground

The foreground is down in front, and everything here is more detailed and larger. Use heavier fabric pieces and work with thicker threads and yarns to create detailed stitches. Place the heavy embellishments in the foreground.

The Color Rule

Color helps indicate depth because darks recede and lights come forward. Keep the background dark and lighten the foreground to create more depth. I use this rule as a safety net. Mother Nature doesn't obey this rule, as distant backgrounds are often grayed and hazy!

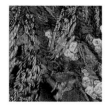

Big Sur in May, 11″ × 16″, **Private Collection**

Big Sur, California, is beautiful at any time of the year, but in the springtime the wildflowers add to the beauty of the pounding surf and breathtaking cliffs. I came across this mass of wildflowers just before the Bixby Bridge.

Materials: Hand-dyed silk, cotton, cheesecloth, netting, tulle, velvet, mohair yarns, Montano Series silk threads and ribbons, and pearl cotton threads. Techniques include crazy quilting, silk ribbon embroidery, felting, and free-form embroidery.

V and S Lines

The V Shape

A valley landscape catches the eye because the valley walls form a V, drawing the eye into the center of the painting. The V shape can be an opening in the trees, hills, or mountains, or a cottage pathway.

The S Shape

A road, path, or river curving in an S shape from the foreground into the midground and background will draw in the viewer. This is an easy way to add movement to a landscape.

Use both of these methods to create more emphasis in your landscapes, seascapes, and underwater projects.

Wahatoyas West Peak in August, 14½" × 19",
Courtesy of Megan Brode

The Wahatoyas, also known as the Spanish Peaks, can be seen for miles around, and they decorate my backyard. This landscape features the West Peak, as seen from the valley hayfields.

Materials: Hand-dyed silk, cotton, cheesecloth, netting, tulle, velvet, mohair yarns, Montano Series silk threads and ribbons, and pearl cotton threads. Techniques include crazy quilting, silk ribbon embroidery, felting, and free-form embroidery.

Hints on Water

Large expanses of water lie in flat horizontal lines. The line dividing the sky and the water (sea, ocean, and so on) becomes the horizon line.

- Calm water acts as a mirror, reflecting the images along banks and shorelines. Water also reflects shadows.

- Earth and stone banks contain rivers and streams—the bank fabric lies over the river fabric to contain it. This helps the viewer make sense of the painting.

- The waves of the sea and large lakes roll in over the beach—the water fabric will lie over the beach fabric to indicate the back-and-forth motion of the waves.

- Many times water and sky can be formed from one fabric. When pressing the seamline, press the seam allowance under the water, so that the bump side is the water—this puts the sky behind the water.

- Organza and netting work well with water and sky, as they add depth and sheen to the painting.

Detail of *On the Road to Seward* (next page). Shadows are created from layers of hand-dyed organza and cheesecloth overlaid with layers of organza.

Detail of *Big Sur in May* (pages 102 and 103). Water is created with crazy-quilt piecing overlaid with hand-dyed silk organzas.

On the Road to Seward, 10″ × 14½″, Private Collection

While driving on the road to Seward, Alaska, in July, I was amazed to see a lake filled with yellow water lilies! The vivid greens of the marsh grasses and the deep tones of the evergreens made the yellow even brighter. I later discovered that the yellow pond lily (*Nuphar polysepalum*) dots many lakes and ponds throughout Alaska.

Materials: Hand-dyed silk organza, tulle, cheesecloth, and cotton fabrics, and Montano Series variegated silk threads and ribbons. Techniques include silk ribbon embroidery, felting, and free-form embroidery.

Creating Underwater Projects

The rules of painting apply to underwater projects as well. The light source is overhead, and air is replaced with water. There are hills, valleys, cliffs, and plains along with a foreground, midground, and background, all under the sea. Seaweed and kelp, anchored to rocks and corals, wave and swirl in the water currents, reaching up to the light. Fish and unanchored organisms float throughout the water. It is a busy place with lots of movement.

There is a horizon line under the sea, and it is just as important as in a landscape or seascape. Important points to remember include the following:

- If the horizon line is above the center, there will be more midground and foreground and less background. This allows more room for free-form stitching and embellishing, giving the stitcher more leeway in adding texture and detail.

- If the horizon line lies below the center of a project, there will be less midground and foreground and more background, creating less space for detail stitches and embellishments. The sky or background will be much larger and important!

- Organisms under the sea attach themselves to rocky and coral berms on the bottom and tend to float upward. So make the horizon line lower to allow for all the upward-floating shapes.

Under the Sea, 12" × 18", **Private Collection**

The sea anemones and starfish that live among the rugged rocks of the Monterey coastline are beautiful and fascinating to me. I love creating underwater projects because I can use so many different needlework techniques and materials.

Materials: Hand-dyed silk, cotton, velvet, cheesecloth, organza, netting, and scrim, along with silk and organza ribbons, fancy yarns, variegated threads, silk tubing, mulberry bark, Montano Series silk threads and ribbons, beads, shells, buttons, metallic threads, and beach findings.

Detail photos on this page from *Sea Garden* (next page)

Twisted organza ribbon can be anchored down with beads and stitches. Wire ribbon can be scrunched and attached with silk ribbon floral stitches. Buttons, tiny seashells, and unusual beads can be clustered to create the illusion of stones and texture. Lace, stressed and frayed at the edges, becomes a sea coral. The underwater projects allow for more embellishments.

For me, underwater projects are more free-form than landscapes or seascapes because I do not work from actual photographs. I work from my sketches and personal photos of beach things, and I refer to underwater shapes in books and magazines. I keep files on all types of jellyfish, anemones, algae, fish, and seaweed for reference.

The same rules of painting still apply, but it is murky and eerie down there. The distance is hazed, so I use burned layers of organza ribbons for seaweed shapes. Where they overlap creates more shapes and shadows. I use several layers of netting or tulle to hold some of the fish shapes and seaweed shapes in place. The layers help haze things down and create a mood.

Sea Garden, 14″ × 24″, Private Collection

To celebrate my 50th birthday, I took diving lessons on the Great Barrier Reef, near Cairns, Queensland, Australia. The sea gardens were breathtakingly beautiful, and I have been creating them in fabric and threads ever since! I love creating underwater scenes, as they are colorful and detailed.

Materials: I used hand-dyed silk, cotton, velvet, cheesecloth, organza, netting, scrim, silk and organza ribbons, fancy yarns, variegated threads, silk findings, mulberry bark, Montano Series silk threads and ribbons, beads, shells, buttons, metallic threads, and tubing.

Monterey Kelp Beds, 15″ × 26″, Private Collection

The Monterey area is so beautiful, and I enjoy going to the Monterey Bay Aquarium to view the jellyfish collection and the kelp tanks. This project was deeply influenced by these visits.

Materials: I used hand-dyed silk, cotton, velvet, cheesecloth, organza, netting, scrim, silk and organza ribbons, fancy yarns, variegated threads, silk tubing, mulberry bark, Montano Series silk threads and ribbons, beads, shells, buttons, metallic threads, and beach findings.

Felting

Felting is a very old technique that has been revived in the textile art world. A single barbed needle is used to punch or force one material into another. An embellisher takes most of the work out of felting. I first used one in a Jan Beaney and Jean Littlejohn class, and on my return home I purchased a Baby Lock 7 needle embellisher. I use the embellisher to hold things in place more than to felt. This saves me hours of time in tacking and lets me get to the free-form embroidery. It also lets me create shapes with extra texture.

Magic Carpet Ride, 18″ × 23″, Private Collection

This project is a mixed-media challenge using black wool backing embellished with felted velvet insets. The wool was stamped with metallic paints and then embellished with long running stitches and herringbone stitches. It was made during a Jan Beaney and Jean Littlejohn seminar.

Materials: I used wool fabric and hand-dyed silk velvets, Robert Gill paints, and Montano variegated threads, and I embellished the piece with an embellisher.

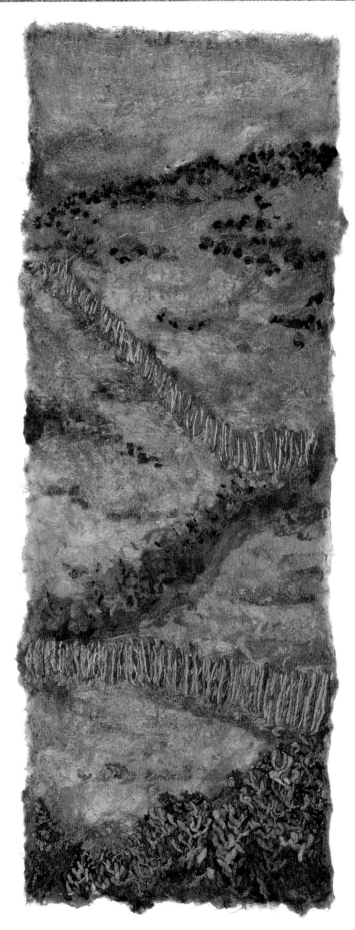

Sometimes I want to create a background design, and the embellisher gives me this freedom. I can add various shapes to a wholecloth backing with the embellisher and then hand embroider on top. Using a soft open-weave fabric for the backing helps in the embellishing. Many times I work the layers of embroidery stitches and then notice that stitches in the background and midground do not recede enough. By carefully going over them with the embellisher I can push them back. It helps embed the stitches into the fabric and gives a feeling of depth.

Pinion Pine, Coyote Fence, and Rabbit Brush,
10″ × 22″, **Private Collection**

Northern New Mexico is crisscrossed with rustic coyote fences (made from rough juniper or aspen poles or branches), dotted with sturdy pinion pines, and decorated with the yellow blooming rabbit brush. Sheep and goats abound, along with many breeds of cattle. This project was created during a Santa Fe seminar with Jan Beaney and Jean Littlejohn. It is the beginning of a series.

Materials: The background is handmade fabric created from wool and silk roving. The trees are created from wool embroidery and felting. The fence line is worsted wool (made from northern New Mexico sheep) and embroidered straight stitches.

LAGUNA PUEBLO

The Laguna Pueblo in March, 24″ × 16″, Private Collection

Laguna is a Native American tribe of the Pueblo people who are situated in the central western part of New Mexico. The Spanish built the Mission San José de la Laguna in 1699. It sits at the top of the pueblo, and the gleaming white adobe walls can be seen for miles around.

Materials: I used hand-dyed silks, cottons, and velvets; netting, tulle, organza, cheesecloth, and scrim make up the sky. The embroidery materials include wool yarns, various silk threads, silk ribbons, and linen.

The Laguna Pueblo project came about because of a March road trip with my husband, Ernest. We were returning from Sedona, Arizona, when we came upon a late afternoon rainstorm. The skies were filled with dramatic, billowing clouds, and it was pelting down.

Just as we approached the Laguna pueblo off Highway I-40, 45 miles west of Albuquerque, the storm eased up, and suddenly great shafts of light were streaking through the clouds. We pulled off the highway and drove toward the pueblo. I took several photos, but the best was when I captured a raven in midflight, riding the air currents. After a while we drove into the pueblo so that I could take some detail shots. I could hardly wait to get home to start my new project. Never mind all the other projects waiting in the studio—this was the one!

Take a creative journey with me as I walk you through the process of creating a textile landscape. From photograph to finished project, I will guide you through the steps and teach you to think like a painter. The Laguna Pueblo project featured in this chapter is for inspiration only, and it demonstrates the general principles put forward in this book. I hope that you will be inspired to create your own free-form embroidery land- or seascape.

Photo Preparation

The computer is a great working tool, and I use it to prepare the basic steps for my landscapes and seascapes.

1. After downloading photos onto my computer, I process them using Adobe Photoshop CS3, choose the one I want, and size it to 24″ × 16″. I make sure the selected photo is a good, clear image and resize it to 300 ppi (pixels per inch).

2. I always make working copies of my original photos by renaming them. For the Laguna Pueblo project, the working copy is named LagunaPueblo24x16.tif. I keep a printout of the photo on the studio table throughout the process. My original photo is filed away for safety on my photography hard drive.

Original photo, LagunaPueblo24x16.tif

3. I alter the photo with the *Palette Knife* filter. This creates a painterly effect with larger blocks of color. This version of the photo is saved as LagunaPuebloPalet24x16.tif. I use this photo for reference when choosing my materials and for blocking in the background, midground, and foreground.

Adjusted photo, saved as LagunaPuebloPalet24x16.tif

4. I use the *Find Edges* filter in Photoshop to create an outline sketch of my photo so I can use it for tracing the important lines onto tracing paper. This third version of the photo is saved as LagunaPueblo24x16edges.tif. The *Find Edges* copy looks like an outline and a negative.

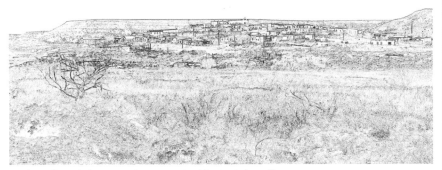

Further adjusted photo, saved as LagunaPueblo24x16edges.tif

Now I have three versions of my original photo. I print them out in the 24″ × 16″ size. This helps me keep everything in proportion. Usually I make a tracing from the *Find Edges* copy, but this time the *Find Edges* copy is so clear that I work directly from it. I do keep tracing paper on the table for making patterns.

Making Patterns

I make traced paper pattern pieces for landscape formations that need to be accurate. A well-known mountain, hill, or valley needs to be recognizable. I place the tracing paper over my *Find Edges* photograph and do a very detailed trace using pencil and then ink. I number all the pieces starting in the background, working forward into the midground and foreground.

To make a pattern, I simply place tracing paper over the desired shape and draw the shape in pencil. I then cut out the shape, making sure to cut on the *out*side of the line. I always add about ⅛″ on the bottom of the pattern piece, as it will tuck under the next shape in front of it. It is then pinned to fabric and cut out. The fabric edges are then burned down to the drawn line.

Selecting a Mat

Painters use mats or frames to view their projects as they work. A mat acts as a barrier and contains the picture, allowing the artist to see what the actual picture will look like. It also helps the artist check whether the perspective is correct.

For this project, I purchased a working mat (page 21) in a neutral color, with an inside measurement of 24″ × 16″. Working mats are used throughout the process and get rather messy. I keep several of these working mats in my studio for other projects.

Note

Keep a small mirror at hand as you work along. When you look through the mirror at the project you will see a reverse image, and this instantly shows any problems.

Fabric Layers

Because painting is like a backward journey (starting from the most distant point and working forward), I use the same procedure in laying down the first layer of fabrics. To make the process easier, I number specific sections on the trace or *Find Edges* copy, starting from the farthest point back (the sky will be #1) and then working forward. This helps me place the fabric pieces in the correct order.

✦ *Worktable Tip*

I always work under good light, in this case Ott lights. I keep a small container of sharp scissors, needles, gluestick, Nymo thread, and tweezers on the worktable.

As I work from the background to the midground, I always check the pattern placement. I do this by laying down the whole trace pattern and making small pencil marks onto the fabrics already in place. I also keep a ruler on my desk for checking out measurements. Because there are so many buildings in this project I really had to pay attention. I use a gluestick to temporarily hold the fabric pieces in place, and then I use small running stitches with a fine thread to hold the pieces to the backing. Also, I do not move forward to the midground until the background pieces are stitched down.

Notice in the photo (below) that the burned edges of the background mesa are covered with a layer of netting. I do this to haze out the background and to push it back. I burn the edges to create a more organic shape.

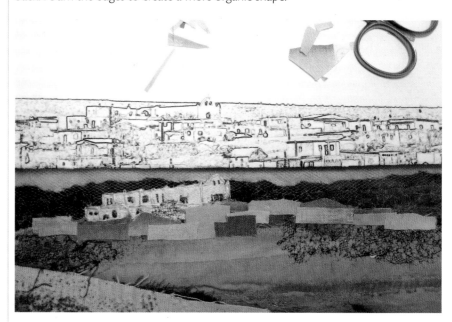

✦ *Working with Small Pieces*

It is difficult to appliqué small and undulating fabric pieces. You can create a better effect and more accurate line by burning the fabric edge. Hold the fabric pattern piece to a candle flame. The edge becomes charred and creates a darker edge, which looks like a charcoal or pencil line. Frayed edges are not a problem, as the project will be framed under glass. Various types of fabrics burn differently, and each has a different type of edge.

- Cottons flame up more than other fabrics, and the burned edge will be black.

- Silk is the easiest to control—it takes on a beautiful brown edge and will not flame up.

- Polyester fabrics will melt when held to a flame and form a beaded hard black edge.

Hold the fabric steady in the flame. Don't wave it about. Each time you hold it to the flame, pinch the edge of the fabric to prevent it from smoldering or flaring up.

Texture works only in the midground and the foreground. Everything in the background is far away and small. Fine threads can indicate a tree line, or perhaps one layer of organza could indicate a line of hills. The stitch lines act as drawing lines and tack the background shapes in place. You can see lines of stitching in the background mesa.

In the photo below, you can see that all the base pieces have been placed. The background is behind the netting, and a few pieces of netting and tulle have been embellished with the Baby Lock embellisher. Now it is time to pin the project up on the corkboard for observation before I continue with the next layers.

Wrinkled, pleated, and manipulated fabrics placed in the foreground create depth and interest. Silk fabrics work best, so use them in the foreground to indicate hills, cliffs, and rock formations.

This valley in the midsection may be a good place for some crazy quilting. I like the challenge of incorporating crazy quilting into a landscape or seascape. In the Laguna project, it represents the valley in the midsection. The challenge is to keep the crazy-quilt pieces directional and to choose pieces that will "paint" for you. I chose fabrics to create light and shadow for the crazy-quilt section.

Texture is felted into the midground and the foreground with bits of hand-dyed silk organza, cheesecloth, and scrim. Black and brown netting is felted into place to create shadows and a background for free-form stitching. Now that the overall fabric pieces are tacked in place, the project is ready for layers of embroidery stitching.

Stitched Layers

It is time to start the backward journey again! I select the embroidery threads for the background and complete this area before going to the midground. The new stitches and embellishments in the midground will cover some previous stitching in the background—this creates the illusion of distance.

Creating Depth

Think about creating a shrub. The trunk and main branches are embroidered first and then the smaller branches and twigs. Next come leaves and then the flowers. Everything is layered, with stitches covering some of the previous layers. These steps will make a realistic-looking shrub, and the eye will see all the layers. Remember that you are thinking like a painter.

Lines of stitching can be used to suggest crags and crannies in the background. They can indicate waves in the ocean or glimmers of light reflecting off the water. Remember that even the background is worked in layers (constantly think: background, midground, and foreground).

Start adding a bit more detail in the midground area. Use the featherstitch and straight stitch to create shrubs and trees. Knotted stitches can be clustered to indicate rock outcroppings or fields of flowers. Work these stitches over the felted cheesecloth, scrim, and netting.

Complete the midground area before you move on to the foreground, because the stitchery and embellishments in the foreground will cover parts of the midground and background.

Working in the foreground is a satisfying part of the whole process with landscapes and seascapes because the work is more layered and detailed. (Some of my pieces are up to four inches deep at the very front of the foreground.) Once again, keep thinking background, midground, and foreground.

Stepping Back to Take a Look

It is hard to see your mistakes if you do not look up from your work, so I like to take a break from my project for a day or two. I pin it to the corkboard with the mat in place. This way I can view it as I walk about the studio. I check it out with a mirror to see the reverse image, and I like to glance at it as I go by. Usually something jumps out, calling for correction.

Many times when I am working on the project at the table I will turn it upside down to see if it is balanced.

Grasses and Shrubs

The grass layers in the foreground are tacked in place with the embellisher. I use hand-dyed silk velvets, crinkled silk organza, cheesecloth, and scrim.

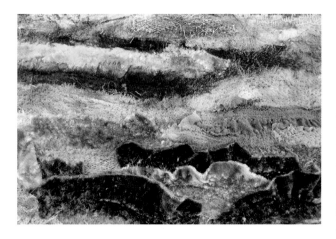

As I build it up, I lose more and more of the crazy-quilt section! I am intent on placing the grass and weeds, and it seems the crazy-quilt section is too colorful for that area. The only way to calm it down is to start over or to cover it with stitching.

Even shrubs have a background, midground, and foreground. I want to keep the velvet shrub pieces loose on the top to give the feeling of depth.

In order to build up the valley of grasses and shrubs, I need to lay down background threads and texture. I use layers of stitches—featherstitch, straight stitch, fly stitch, and coral stitch—in various weights of thread and yarn.

The left-hand corner is built up with wrinkled hand-dyed cheesecloth. To create more depth, I place a padded piece of felt under the wrinkled cheesecloth. Velvet shapes are tacked into place, forming the base for evergreen shrubs.

Foreground

The foreground is now ready for completion. The background and midground are filled in, and I am satisfied with the results.

I make a *Find Edges* (page 117) print of a white tree that was growing by the roadside. I want to use it in the foreground to create interest and depth. Because the photo was taken in March, the grass is brown and the trees are bare. I have to make the tree and the fallen tree trunk interesting, so I use hand-dyed silk ribbon in a split stitch and then go over it with simple embroidery stitches. The starkness of the tree adds depth.

The Laguna project was a big challenge, as I had never worked with so many buildings—nor had I worked with such a vast, barren-looking landscape. It was a challenge to stay within the range of a New Mexico winter scene. I kept reaching for brighter and more intense colors!

It was also a challenge to keep it real, just like the photograph, which shows an ancient, tumbled-down but proud Indian reservation topped by Mission San José de la Laguna. This mission was erected by the Spanish in 1699 and dominates the hillside of the old pueblo, now Old Laguna. It is like looking back in time.

I have great admiration for the Laguna (*Kawaik* in Western Keres) people and their history. They are the largest Keresan-speaking tribe, at more than 7,000 people. Over the years the old buildings clinging to the hillside and the vastness of the New Mexico valley have intrigued me. It reminds me of the old villages in Spain.

The name *Laguna* means "lake" in Spanish, but there is no lake to be seen from the highway. The rocky plateaus, high desert growth, and vast skies offer up a panorama of Southwest romance and reality.

Source Guide

Products

Artimis
www.artemisinc.com
888-233-5187
Hand-dyed silk ribbons for embroidery, crafting, and fashion

Art Van Go, the Studios
www.artvango.co.uk
+44 (0)-1438-814946
(United Kingdom)
Wonderful sources for all types of arts and crafts

Baby Lock
www.babylock.com
Embellishers (felting machines) and sewing machines

Bernina
www.berninausa.com
Sewing machines

Colour Streams
www.colourstreams.com.au
+61 2-6684-2577
(Australia)
Amazing hand-dyed silk ribbons, threads, batts, and specialty fabrics, and products for hand embroidery and textile art

Dharma Trading Co.
www.dharmatrading.com
800-542-5227
Dyes, paints, silk fabrics, transfer products, books, tools, resists, markers, clothing blanks, and PFD (prepared for dyeing) fabrics

Double Trouble Enterprises
www.doubletrouble-ent.com
fax: +44 (0)-1628-675699
(United Kingdom)
Home of international needlework team Jan Beaney and Jean Littlejohn; wonderful books, DVDs, and a source of suppliers and links

Fabric Painting by Ginny Eckley
www.fabricpainting.com
281-358-2951
Colorhue dyes, books, DVDs, stencils, and scarf blanks. Ginny is an internationally recognized fiber artist and teacher.

Flights of Fancy Inc.
www.flightsoffancyboutique.com
800-530-8745
Trims, embellishments, books, patterns, and kits for stamping and crafting—a wonderful treasure trove

Golden Thread Silks
www.goldenthreadsilks.com
530-344-1828
Handwoven, naturally dyed silks from Vietnam, Cambodia, and Laos

Joggles.com
www.joggles.com
401-615-7696
Everything you will need for textile art, cloth dolls, and mixed-media art projects

Judith Designs
www.judithbakermontano.com
719-742-3388
Books, artwork, and site for Judith's Studio Seminars

Kreinik
www.kreinik.com
800-537-2166
Beautiful metallic threads for machine and hand embroidery

Leilani Arts
www.leilaniarts.net
808-298-3208
Exotic yarns, fibers, textiles, and beads; wonderful silk, and silk sari yarns

M'Art Designs
www.m-artistic.com
Beautiful hand-dyed fabrics by artist Marit Lee Kucera

Mary Fisher Productions, Inc.
www.maryfisher.com
928-282-5960
Beautiful prints, handmade paper, fiber art, sculpture, bracelets from the Abataka Collection

Mokuba Ribbons
www.mokubany.com
212-869-8900
Wonderful ribbons of all types

Nordic Needle Inc.
www.nordicneedle.com
800-433-4321
Wonderful store and catalog for all types of needlework

Painter's Threads Collection
www.paintersthreads.eu
www.tentakulum.de
fax: +49 (0)-69-60607033
(Germany)
Amazing source for hand-dyed threads, textile papers, silk rovings, and cocoons

QuiltingArts.com
www.quiltingarts.com
800-272-2193
Books, magazines, supplies for needlework and fiber art

Robert Kaufman Fabrics
www.robertkaufman.com
Wonderful fabrics for fiber art; maker of Radiance, a cotton/silk blend

Robert Talbott Carmel
www.roberttalbott.com
888-557-0575
Great outlet for Italian silk, used in the famous ties

Sara's Bloom
www.sarabloom.com
949-651-8484
Lace, metallic trims, ribbons, trims, fringes, rayon lace dyes, and brushes

Skydyes
www.skydyes.com
860-232-1429
Books, paints, and hand-painted cottons and silks. Mickey Lawler is famous for her beautiful fabrics that suggest skies and landscapes.

Stef Francis
www.stef-francis.co.uk
+44 (0)-1803-323004
(United Kingdom)
Wonderful space-dyed silk threads, yarns, ribbons, fabrics, and silk findings

Stewart Gill
www.stewartgill.com
+44 (0)-1383-842200
(United Kingdom)
Wonderful textile paints with a full line of colors and beautiful stencils

St. Theresa Textile Trove
www.sttheresatextile.com
859-380-2833
African artifacts, beads, fabrics, trims, and jewelry findings

Superior Threads
www.superiorthreads.com
800-499-1777
Supplier of fine threads in cotton and silk, in variegated colors, and silk ribbons

Susan Clarke Originals
www.susanclarkeoriginals.com
530-246 8880
Buttons, charms, glass, and enamel

Thai Silks
www.thaisilks.com
800-722-7455
More than 1,400 silk fabrics of every kind; blank scarves and artist items

The Thread Studio
www.thethreadstudio.com
+61 8-9227-1561
(Australia)
Amazing and unusual threads; everything for textile art, online workshops, and books (orders by phone or email only)

Treenway Silks
www.treenwaysilks.com
888-383-7455
Silk ribbon, threads, many unusual silk products; Montano Series of variegated silk threads and ribbons

YLI Corporation
www.ylicorp.com
803-985-3100
A wonderful variety of threads in silk, rayon, nylon, metallic, and cotton for embroidery, quilting, sewing, serging, and embellishing

Schools and Associations

City and Guilds
www.cityandguilds.com/uk
(United Kingdom)

Constance Howard Resource and Research Centre in Textiles
www.gold.ac.uk/constance-howard
+44 (0)-2077-172210
(United Kingdom)

Embroiderers' Guild
www.embroderersguild.com
+44 (0)-1932-260738
(United Kingdom)

Gail Harker Creative Studies Center
www.gailcreativestudies.com
360-279-2105

Royal School of Needlework
www.royal-needlework.org.uk
+44 (0)-2031-666932
(United Kingdom)

School of Stitched Textiles
www.sofst.org
+44 (0)-1257-463163
(United Kingdom)

Surface Design Association
www.surfacedesign.org
707-829-3110

Windsor School of Textile Arts (East Berkshire College)
www.eastberks.ac.uk
+44 (0)-1753-793000
(United Kingdom)

Artists, Teachers, and More Inspiration

The 62 Group
www.62group.org.uk

Barbara Lee Smith
www.barbaraleesmith.com

Carol Shinn
www.carolshinn.com

Erica Wilson and Vladimir Kagan
www.ericawilson.com

www.nantuckettodayonline.com
(under Archives, click "Revisit past issues" > "Nov./Dec. 2008" > "Creatively Kagan")

www.theselby.com (under Manhattan, click "erica wilson & vladimir kagan")
Wonderful photos of Erica Wilson's New York apartment

Jan Beaney and Jean Littlejohn
www.doubletrouble-ent.com

Kaffe Fassett
www.kaffefassett.com

Mary Corbet's Needle 'n Thread
www.needlenthread.com
Wonderful, informative website

Selvedge **Magazine**
www.selvedge.org

Textile Arts
www.textilearts.net

Verina Warren
www.verinawarren.co.uk

Books

Beaney, Jan. *The Art of the Needle: Designing in Fabric and Threads.* London: Century Hutchinson, 1988.

Beaney, Jan. *Stitches: New Approaches.* London: Batsford, 2004.

Beaney, Jan, and Jean Littlejohn. *A Complete Guide to Creative Embroidery: Designs • Textures • Stitches.* London: Batsford, 2003.

Beaney, Jan, and Jean Littlejohn. *Stitch Magic: Ideas and Interpretation.* London: Batsford, 2005.

Box, Richard. *Color and Design for Embroidery.* Dulles, VA: Brassey's Inc., 2000.

Box, Richard. *The Embroidered Countryside.* London: Batsford, 1995.

Box, Richard. *Flowers for Embroidery: A Step-by-Step Approach.* London: Batsford, 1993.

Brickell, Christopher, and H. Marc Cathey, eds. *The American Horticultural A–Z Encyclopedia of Garden Plants.* New York: DK Publishing, Inc. 1996.

Brown, Pauline. *Decoration on Fabric: A Sourcebook of Ideas.* London: Guild of Master Craftsman Publications, 2002.

Embroiderers' Guild, The. *Embroidery Studio—The Ultimate Workshop: Design, Technique and Inspiration.* Newton Abbot, UK: David and Charles, 1996.

Fassett, Kaffe. *Kaffe Fassett's Glorious Color for Needlepoint and Knitting.* New York: Sterling Publishing Company, Inc., 2000.

Fassett, Kaffe. *Glorious Inspirations: Sources from Art and Nature for Innovative Needlework Designs.* New York: Clarkson Potter Publishers, 1991.

Fassett, Kaffe. *Glorious Needlepoint.* New York: Three Rivers Press, 1992.

Fassett, Kaffe, and Candace Bahouth. *Mosaics: Inspiration and 24 Original Projects for Interiors and Exteriors.* Newtown, CT: The Taunton Press, Inc., 2001.

Fassett, Kaffe, with Liza Prior Lucy. *Glorious Patchwork: More Than 25 Glorious Quilt Designs.* New York: Clarkson Potter Publishers, 1997.

Grey, Maggie. *From Image to Stitch.* London: Batsford, 2008.

Grier, Rosey, and Dennis Baker. *Rosey, an Autobiography: The Gentle Giant.* Tulsa, OK: Honor Books, 1986.

Hall, Jane. *The Art and Embroidery of Jane Hall: Reflections of Nature.* Turnbridge Wells, UK: Search Press Ltd., 2010.

Hedley, Gwen. *Drawn to Stitch: Line, Drawing, and Mark-Making in Textile Art.* Loveland, CO: Interweave Press, 2010.

Howard, Constance. *The Constance Howard Book of Stitches.* London: Batsford, 2005.

Howard, Constance. *Embroidery and Colour.* London: Batsford, 1976.

Kahn, Sherrill. *Creative Embellishments for Paper, Jewelry, Fabric, and More.* Woodinville, WA: Martingale & Company, 2007.

Langford, Pat. *Embroidery from Sketch to Stitch.* Cammeray, Australia: Simon & Schuster Australia, 2001.

Lees, Wendy. *Inspired to Stitch: The Creative Embroidery Course.* Newton Abbot, UK: David and Charles, 1994.

Macoboy, Stirling. *Stirling Macoboy's What Flower Is That?* Edison, NJ: Chartwell Books, 2000.

Meech, Sandra. *Connecting Art to Stitch.* London: Batsford, 2009.

Meech, Sandra. *Contemporary Quilts: Design, Surface and Stitch.* London: Batsford, 2007.

Mein, Annemieke. *The Art of Annemieke Mein: Wildlife Artist in Textiles.* Turnbridge Wells, UK: Search Press Ltd., 2008.

Shinn, Carol. *Freestyle Machine Embroidery: Techniques and Inspiration for Fiber Art.* Loveland, CO: Interweave Press, 2009.

Smith, Barbara Lee. *Celebrating the Stitch: Contemporary Embroidery of North America.* Newtown, CT: The Taunton Press, Inc., 1991.

Snyderman, Marty, and M. Tundi Agardy. *Life in the Sea.* Lincolnwood, IL: Publications International, 1997.

Springall, Diana. *Inspired to Stitch: 21 Textile Artists.* London: A&C Black, 2005.

Taylor's Guide to Shrubs (Kathleen Fisher, ed., 2000), *Taylor's Guide to Trees* (Susan A. Roth, ed., 2001), *Taylor's Guide to Natural Gardening* (Roger Holmes, ed., 1993). Based on *Taylor's Encyclopedia of Gardening.* Boston: Houghton Mifflin Company.

Warren, Verina. *Landscape in Embroidery.* London: Batsford, 1990.

Watts, Pamela. *Embroidered Flowers.* London: Batsford, 2003.

Wilson, Erica. *Erica Wilson's Embroidery Book.* New York: Charles Scribner's Sons, 1973.

About the Author

Judith Baker Montano is an award-winning and world-renowned Canadian fiber artist, photographer, author, and teacher who is recognized as the consummate expert in crazy quilting, silk ribbon embroidery, and embellishments.

She grew up on the historic Bar U Ranch in Alberta, Canada. Her love of fabrics and embellishments reflects her Indian, French, and German heritage. She attributes the rich, embellished ethnic influence in her work to living between an Indian reserve and a Hutterite colony where she observed beautiful handicrafts. Living in England, Germany, and Japan for eight years was another profound influence on her artwork and outlook.

Judith attended California State University, Chico, and graduated with a degree in art and journalism. Upon graduation, she painted with the San Francisco Art Guild.

Experimenting with materials and her sewing machine, Judith created the Montano Center Piece Method, a copyright-protected machine method of crazy quilting.

Judith was presented with the Governor General's Centennial Award of Canada in recognition for her artwork as a Canadian living abroad.

She has designed for Butterick/Vogue, Bucilla Company, Mokuba Ribbons of Tokyo, Fox Hill Designs, Treenway Silks, Robert Kaufman Fabrics, Kanagawa, and Mokuba ribbons. Her work has been featured at the Denver Art Museum, Denver, Colorado; Profiles Gallery, Edmonton, Alberta, Canada; The Dairy Barn, Athens, Ohio; Mitskoshi Department Show, Tokyo, Japan; Profiles and Visions, Alberta, Canada; and the La Conner Quilt Museum, La Conner, Washington.

Judith has been a guest artist at countless Australian Stitches and Craft Trade shows and the Tokyo Hobby Shows. Her designs have been featured in many international and national magazines such as *Better Homes and Gardens, Quilts Japan,* and *The Quilt Life.* She has appeared on the *Carol Duval Show, Simply Quilts, The Quilt Show,* and *Good Morning Australia.* She has produced award-winning tutorial videos and DVDs.

Teaching takes her throughout the United States, Canada, Europe, Australia, New Zealand, and Japan. Classes range from clothing design, crazy quilting, embellishments, and mixed media to free-form textile art. Every year, from May to September, Judith offers eight exclusive seminars in her private studio. Visit her website, www.judithbakermontano.com, for more details.

Judith resides in the small town of La Veta, Colorado, a conclave of artists, writers, and musicians. She lives in a restored 1876 cottage with her husband, Ernest Shealy, and an ever-increasing menagerie of pets.

Photo by Ernest Shealy

Also by Judith Baker Montano:

Great Products *from* C&T PUBLISHING

Available at your local retailer or **www.ctpub.com** *or* **800-284-1114**